ABSOLUTELY FABULOUS!

RUTH HANISCH

ABSOLUTELY FABULOUS !

ARCHITECTURE AND FASHION

PRESTEL   Munich · Berlin · London · New York

Front cover: Asymptote, Carlos Miele Flagship Store, New York
Front flap: Ron Arad Associates, Yoshi Yamamoto Store, Tokyo
Back cover: Fashion show Christian Dior, Paris
Back flap: atelier architecture & scenography, Andreas Murkudis Store, Berlin
p. 1: Alain Moatti/Henri Rivière, Jean-Paul Gaultier Haute Couture, Paris
pp. 2-3: Toyo Ito, Tod's Flagship Store, Tokyo
pp. 4-5, 9: Massimiliano Fuksas/Doriana O. Mandrelli, Emporio Armani, Shanghai
p. 7: NL Architects with Droog Design, Mandarina Duck, Paris
p. 8: Renzo Piano Building Workshop, Maison Hermès, Tokyo

© PRESTEL VERLAG,
Munich · Berlin · London · New York
2006

Prestel Verlag
Königinstrasse 9
80539 Munich
Tel. +49 (0)89-38 17 09-0
Fax +49 (0)89-38 17 09-35
www.prestel.de

Prestel Publishing Ltd.
4, Bloomsbury Place
London WC1A 2QA
Tel. +44 (0) 20-73 23-50 04
Fax +44 (0) 20-76 36-80 04

Prestel Publishing
900 Broadway, Suite 603
New York, NY 10003
Tel. +1 (2 12) 9 95-27 20
Fax +1 (2 12) 9 95-27 33
www.prestel.com

Library of Congress Control Number:
2006900787

The Deutsche Bibliothek holds a record of this publication in the Deutsche Nationalbibliografie; detailed bibliographical data can be found under http://dnb.ddb.de

Prestel books are available worldwide. Please contact your nearest bookseller or one of the above addresses for information concerning your local distributor.

Translation from the German: Roderick O'Donovan, Vienna
Editorial direction: Sandra Leitte, Angeli Sachs
Copyediting: Cynthia Hall, Stephanskirchen
Picture research: Sophie Kowall
Cover and design concept: LIQUID Agentur für Gestaltung, Augsburg
Design, layout and typesetting: Cilly Klotz
Origination: ReproLine Genceller, Munich
Printing and binding: Passavia, Passau
Printed in Germany on acid-free paper

ISBN 3-7913-3521-9
978-3-7913-3521-6

PICTURE CREDITS

Front cover: Paul Warchol Photography
Front flap: Nacasa & Partners
Back cover: Madame Figaro/laif
Back flap: Thomas Meyer/Ostkreuz

Nicolas Borel 1
Nacasa & Partners Inc. 2-3
Giacomo Giannini 4-5, 9
Wouter van den Brink 7
Michel Denancé 8
Hertha Hurnaus 10-15
AMO 16-19
Daici Ano, courtesy of Louis Vuitton 20-23
Nacasa & Partners Inc. 24-29
Asymptote 30-31
Paul Warchol Photography 32-33
atelier architecture & scenography, photographs: Thomas Meyer/Ostkreuz 34-37
fotografieSCHAULIN 38
Oliver Heissner 39-41
Morgane Le Galle 42-45
Ramon Prat 46-51
Fuksas Archive 52-53
Nacasa & Partners Inc. 54-57
Donato Dibello 58, 59 above, 60 above, 61 right
Lee Funnell/domus 59 below, 60 below, 61 left
Daici Ano 62-65
Nacasa & Partners 66-69
Roger Casas 70-71
Bauer & Deininger 72-73
Barry S. Laden 74-75
Kazou Ohishi 76-79
Luc Boegly 81-83

Nicolas Borel 84
Sophie Elbaz 85
Wouter van den Brink 86-87
Courtesy of Prada 88-91
Michel Denancé/artur 93-95
CCP/MAK 2003, photographs:
Stefan Zeisle 96-97
Katharina Rohde 98-99
Roberto Cavalli 100-103
SANAA 104-105
Bauer & Deininger 106-107
Shaun Jarvis 108-113
Michael Moran 114-117
Stürm & Wolf 118-120
Paul Warchol Photography 121
Andrea Martiradonna 122-127
the next ENTERprise 128-129
wulf & partner 130 below
adidas, photographs: B. Wiemann 130 above, 131 above
Roland Halbe/artur 131 below, 132-133
Ramon Prat 134-135
Issey Miyake, photograph: Yasuati Yoshinaga 136
Lucy Orta, artist, holds the first Rootstein Hopkins Chair at London College of Fashion, University of the Arts, London, photographs: John Akehurst 137 above, Peter Guenzel 137 below
Graphische Sammlung Albertina, Vienna/Adolf Loos Archiv 139
Studio Ivan Nemec 138
Margherita Spiluttini 140 above
Tadao Ando Architect & Associates 140 below
Ramon Prat 141, 144
Courtesy of Prada 142
Richard Davies 143

Contents

ALLESWIRDGUT

DON GIL BRANCH

This commission involved not only designing a retail outlet for the Don Gil chain but also developing a spatial concept for this men's fashion retailer.

The optimistic young Vienna-based practice Alles-WirdGut (literally: everything will be fine) that explores an expanded definition of architecture made branding into the spatial programme. A "catwalk" was developed as a leitmotif with an instantly recognisable quality, a red band that interprets the Don Gil logo three-dimensionally.

The catwalk makes its most dramatic appearance in the Graz shop in Murgasse. It winds through the entire space, in the process transforming into various parts of the fittings such as the cash desk, the banisters to the staircase and the landings. At first-floor level the start is made by a kind of telescope with an inserted monitor. But this catwalk is not for striding along; it serves instead to explain the spatial structure. The reference to the logo's text is particularly emphatic where negative shapes are cut out of the polyethylene band that at one point forms the logo itself. To give the logo the maximum long-distance effect the façade is completely transparent, with the entrance door indicated only by a metal frame.

The remainder of the fittings are restrained to avoid diminishing the impact made by the catwalk inside the shop. Expensive natural materials in shades of beige form a strong contrast to the pillar-box red of the catwalk. The atmosphere is expansive and relaxed throughout, not only in the lounge, an indispensable feature for every fashion shop with aspirations. Here backlit landscape photography by Austrian artist Hertha Hurnaus introduces nature into the shopping environment. In terms of space and materials the fitting rooms, too, are far more than just sad, leftover spaces. The shop in Murgasse forms part of what has become a good old Austrian tradition of commissioning radical young architects to design shop interiors – the inner city of Vienna is full of such elegant miniatures by architects ranging from Adolf Loos to Hans Hollein.

»10

1|

2|

LOCATION:
Don Gil
Murgasse 1
Graz, Austria
INTERNET:
www.dongil.at

1+2| The façade is rather restrained, in contrast the large logo makes a bold statement.

SHOP MURGASSE

3 | The shop exercises discreet restraint ...
4 + 5 | ... apart, that is, from the red PVC element
that takes many different shapes and forms an
axis around which the spaces are organised.

4 |

Monitor, monitor on the wall... AMO – the think tank of OMA Office for Metropolitan Architecture — developed and implemented a new use of computer technology in the Prada Epicenters in New York and Los Angeles.

So, for example, details of the collections can be retrieved at computer stations in the flagship store, and a magic mirror in the fitting room makes it possible to see oneself from the front and the back at the same time. In harmony with the architectural notion the virtual concept also aims at expanding the definition of shopping. Shopping and surfing – not in the wide expanses of the customary www but in the sheltered regions of an electronic web developed especially for the individual customer. An area reserved for the individual customer on the website where information about purchases and fittings is stored is the equivalent to the privacy of the fitting room. The hardware, too, must be sensibly integrated in the design. Ubiquitous displays hanging between the clothes produced by this cult label offer a witty mix of fashion and technology.

1 |

>> 16

LOCATION:
Prada Epicenters
841 Madison Ave at 70th St.
New York, USA

343 North Rodeo Drive
Los Angeles, CA, USA
INTERNET:
www.prada.com

PRADA IN-STORE TECHNOLOGY

2|

The textures of the clothes are overlaid with the structures on the monitors, at some places complementary, at others contrasting. The contents also often provide a contrast. In addition to stock market figures and advertising or information about the involvement of Prada in cultural and sporting matters, arbitrarily selected fragments about the outside world also crop up, icons of day-to-day life or of art history. This blend of images reflects the architectural leit-motif of the stores in New York and Los Angeles: an attempt to regain space for public culture by means of shopping at a higher level.

3 |

1 | Virtual reality, off the rack.
2+6 | A touch of reality among marvellous materials.
3 | Prada has its finger on the pulse of daily life.
4 | The architects' criticism of consumption.
5 | The monitors are hung, laid, positioned and, at places, framed.

5

In a world where everything is shopping...

and shopping is everything...

what is luxury?

Luxury is NOT shopping.

Luxury

=

Attention

“Rough”

Intelligence

“Waste”

Stability

4

6

1

2

LOUIS

LOCATION:
Louis Vuitton Roppongi
Roppongi Keyakizaka Dori, Roppongi Hills
6-12-3 Roppongi Minato-ku
Tokyo, Japan
INTERNET:
www.vuitton.com

1 | Architecture of the night: in the dark the elevation is part of a mise-en-scène.
2 | The meeting of inside and outside is a leitmotiv of this architecture.
3 | Dematerialisation of the walls is a further theme.
4 | A detail of the glass tubes that form the façade pattern.

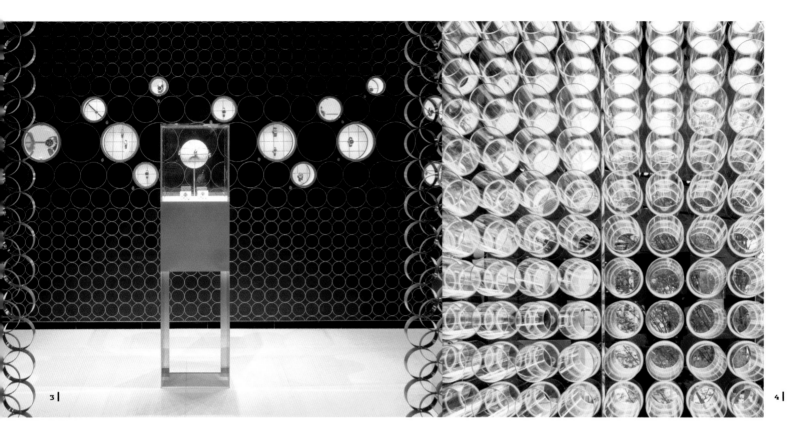

VUITTON

JUN AOKI, ERIC CARLSON, AURELIO CLEMENTI
TOKYO, JAPAN 2003

Louis Vuitton bags are a cult in Japan; in fact many elegant Japanese ladies carry two of these fetish items at the same time.

The presence of the brand in Japanese cities, especially Tokyo, reflects this obsession. In contrast to the Vuitton shop on the famous Tokyo shopping street Omotesando, the shop in the Roppongi Hills stands in the pole position in one of the new mini cities, a huge shopping and entertainment complex in an area known for its nightlife. This explains the slightly risqué mix of bar, lounge, discotheque and shopping. The façade continues the notion of interference that Jun Aoki developed for the first Louis Vuitton shop in Nagoya. In Nagoya two different wall layers were used, one transparent, the other opaque, both of them stamped with

5 |

6 |

›› **22**

the typical Vuitton pattern. The perspective shift between the two planes created a kind of moiré effect.

In the building in the Roppongi Hills in Tokyo a similarly distorting effect is achieved by using over 20,000 glass tubes that project fragmented parts of the interior outwards. The façade resembles a screen on which the countless reflections and refractions from the interior are like pixels that form an understated image of the name of the shop. In the interior the famous Vuitton motif is varied further. The partition walls are made of layers of steel rings that overlap to form the typical Vuitton pattern. The ubiquitous presence of such a motif could be excessive were it not for the fact that, as shoppers move through the store, they register the motif only briefly.

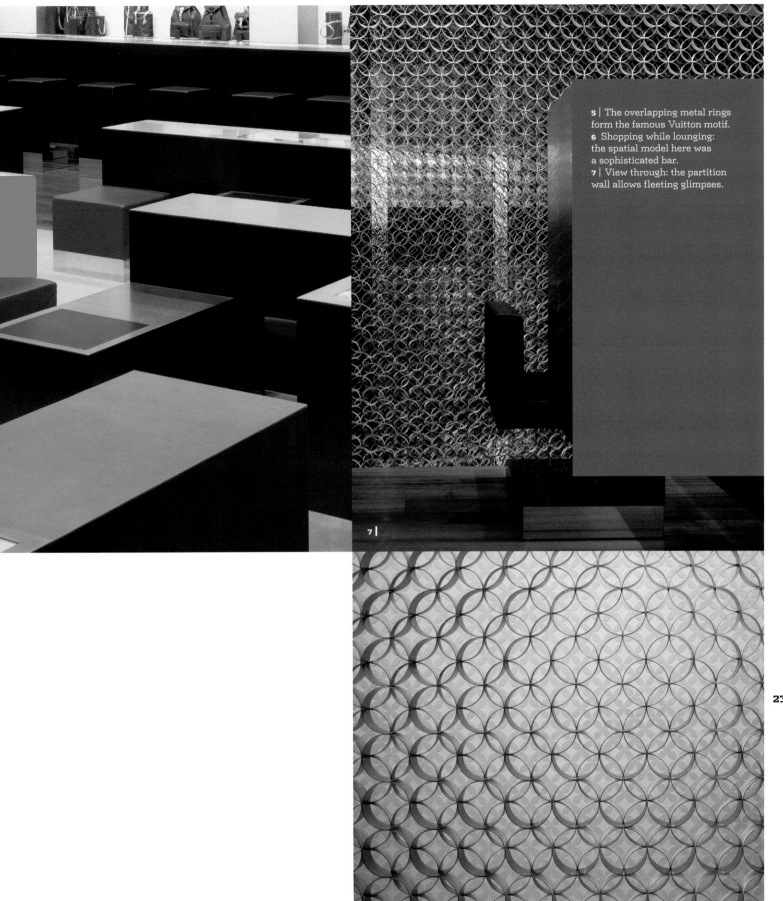

5 | The overlapping metal rings form the famous Vuitton motif.
6 Shopping while lounging: the spatial model here was a sophisticated bar.
7 | View through: the partition wall allows fleeting glimpses.

7 |

1|

Roppongi Hills, the new mini-city or, to put it better, the new maxi shopping centre with cultural aspirations in the west of the metropolis Tokyo contains several of the most interesting new boutiques.

One of these is Yohji Yamamoto's label, Y's. For the casual line of this Japanese fashion creator, architect and designer, Ron Arad developed a presentation mobile. A series of revolving loops made of aluminium tubing were closely packed around the existing pillars, right up to ceiling height. They are pushed tightly against each other and project far into the space. The turntables that are used in garages throughout Tokyo to automatically park cars provided the model for this daring construction. The pieces of clothing can be hung from these aluminium loops or draped across precisely cut, inset shelves. Four of these blocks of stacked, rotating loops structure the space in constantly changing constellations. They are complemented by a mobile stacking shelf system and a kind of banded sales counter. The fitting rooms are concealed behind a wavy wall.

One of Ron Arad's favourite themes is developing the maximum degree of mobility from elements that are, as far as possible, homogeneous and he has varied this theme in numerous designs for useful objects. He thus sits in the same bubble as his teacher at the famous Architectural Association in London, Peter Cook, and Cook's partners in the Archigram group.

›› **24**

1 | View of the door and the moving presentation elements.
2 | The moving bands continuously restructure the space.
3 + 4 | Objects can be hung from, positioned on or laid across the metal bands.

LOCATION:
Y's
Roppongi Keyakizaka-Dori
6-12-4 Roppongi Minato-Ku
Tokyo, Japan
INTERNET:
www.yohjiyamamoto.co.jp

Y'S (YOHJI YAMAMOTO) STORE

3 |

4 |

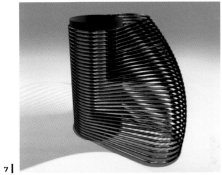

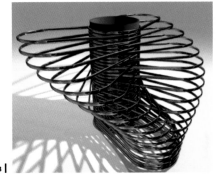

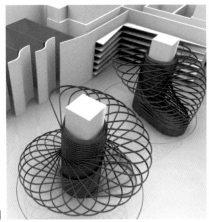

5 | The counter is flexible and layered
in much the same way as the column.
6 | A model of the column at rest ...
7 | ... in ordered motion ...
8 + 9 | ... and completely open.

5 |

6 |

7 |

8 |

9 |

The interior of the Carlos Miele flagship store in New York is curving, rhythmic and shimmering white.

The use of the most modern computer technology made it possible to translate the elegant and mathematically complex folds of heavy silk satin to flll the space. Carlos Miele, Brazil's most famous fashion designer, uses a lavish range of elements: colours, lace, frills and, above all, bouncy flounces at all ends.

Asymptote, the working partnership of Lise Anne Couture and Hani Rashid, is one of the leaders in the area of computer-assisted design, which allows them to form the most geometrically complex surfaces and curves. In this New York project they have developed a presentation framework that allows the buoyantly mobile nature of models to resonate in space and yet retains a strong independence to cope with the changing collections. From outside already one can see through a simple glass façade the free flowing curves and openings in a sculptural centrepiece that divides the shop along its entire depth. Benches, tables and consoles grow

CARLOS MIELE FLAGSHIP STORE

ASYMPTOTE | NEW YORK, USA 2003

LOCATION:
Carlos Miele NY Flagship Store
408 West 14th Street
New York, USA
INTERNET:
www.carlosmiele.com.br

out of it almost naturally. If it were not for the shimmering surface one might feel reminded of Hermann Finsterlin and German expressionism. The centrepiece consists of painted bentwood over a rib and gusset substructure that was directly cut by laser according to a CAD drawing. The considerable technical effort involved is not perceptible and the space curves around the models in a most natural and expressive way.

Two video installations integrated into the space show digital art by Asymptote that deals with the relationship between body and space, a further development of works that were shown at Documenta XI and the Venice Biennale 2004.

1+2 | Tailor-made on the computer: asymmetrical curves at and around the clothes.

3 | A partition wall undulates along the length of the space.
4 | Lighting and subtly differentiated surfaces emphasise the movement.

The boundary between art and fashion is becoming increasingly blurred. Designers tend to curate their boutiques like galleries, and the Murkudis brothers are a duo that embodies this type precisely.

LOCATION:
Andreas Murkudis
Münzstraße 21
Berlin, Germany

Andreas Murkudis is a retailer in Berlin, his brother Kostas works as a fashion designer in Munich. For his Berlin shops Andreas Murkudis chooses "beautiful things" from the collections of various fashion designers, including pieces by his brother, and presents them like artworks in specially designed sales spaces.

The spatial concept of the young Berlin architects Pierre Jorge Gonzales and Judith Haase responds to this scenario. Not by chance their practice has become known principally for its gallery spaces in New York, Paris and Berlin. A few strong elements such as the elongated blue presentation modules and a partition wall with integrated clothes rail focus the gaze on the items of clothing and articulate the long L-shaped space of AM2. The shop is in a rear courtyard in Berlin-Mitte, such premises once usually housed small

1 The entrance, left unchanged, tends to suggest that one is entering a gallery.
2 | Reduced to the max.

AM2 ANDREAS MURKUDIS STORE

3 |

>> **36** workshops or storerooms. There is no advertising on the street front, Murkudis relies on his international clientele to spread his reputation by word-of-mouth. In a discrete manner the team of architects has integrated in their conversion elements such as the old windows with their grilles and the existing tiling, thus further strengthening the SoHo feeling.

Despite the shabby chic atmosphere of this location, the gleaming white paint, the hidden but brilliant lighting and the concealed installations make the room into a "white cube" for carefully selected objects. "Everything that I sell here my family and my friends would like to have themselves", says Andreas Murkudis about his shop.

3 | Plenty of space is created for
the individual objects.
4 | A strongly coloured podium dominates
the sales space.
5 | Minimal differences heighten the excitement.

Blauraum Architekten developed in Hamburg a prototype for further flagship stores for the Swiss bag manufacturer, Freitag, in the form of a box within a box.

LOCATION:
Freitag - The Real F-Shop
Klosterwall 9
Hamburg, Germany
INTERNET:
www.freitag.ch

An opened container with proportions similar to those of the truck trailer takes up almost the whole interior of the elongated glazed building. Inside the container an entire wall is filled with cardboard boxes whose inspection panels offer a first view of the cult bags.

The Freitag bag thus occupies the centre of the architectural concept of the young Hamburg practice. Daniel and Markus Freitag from Zurich sewed the first prototypes of the hardwearing bicycle bag made of recycled truck tarpaulins, car belts and bicycle tubes in 1993. Their intelligent concept survived even its roaring success among the young and young at heart with little damage. The architecture takes up important elements of these unmistakeable bags such as individuality, flexibility and durability, and develops them further. The architects' delight in working out details and in using familiar materials in unusual contexts is impossible to overlook.

1 | The mirror and the view of the street create a moment of spatial confusion.
2 | Looking into the box in the box.

1 |

4 |

3 | The freestanding box resembles a truck trailer.

4 | Each one is unique – the Freitag bags are sewn out of used truck tarpaulins.

3 |

A-POC BOUTIQUE (ISSEY MIYAKE)

1|

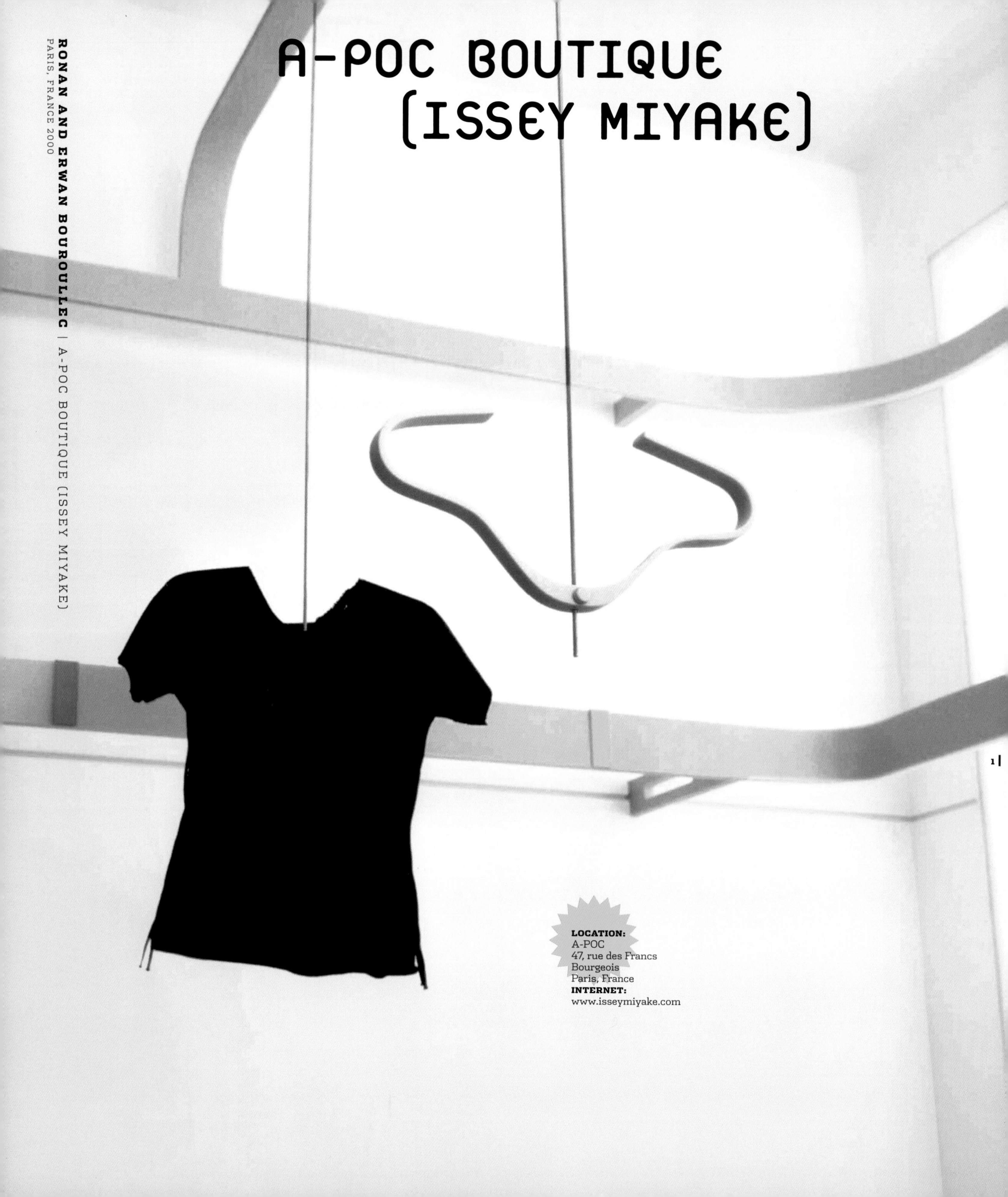

LOCATION:
A-POC
47, rue des Francs
Bourgeois
Paris, France
INTERNET:
www.isseymiyake.com

The design process in this Paris boutique moved from
the clothes hangers to the interior, from small to large, from
direct contact with the clothes to the anchoring in space.

First of all the two brothers designed the elements to hang the clothes on, then the support
system for the hangers. Rails running parallel along the walls cross at ceiling level. This estab-
lishes a system of coordinates that, in principle, means that every point in the space can be used
to present clothes; display is no longer confined to the shop windows or walls. The system is
structurally uniform and at the same time highly flexible. Flat coloured boards can be used horizontally and vertically as additional presentation surfaces for smaller objects, shoes and bags.
Issey Miyake — the Gyro Gearloose of the fashion business — commissioned the two designers,
Ronan and Erwan Bouroullec, to design the sales outlet for his new A-POC range. A-POC stands
for "A Piece Of Cloth" and is a description of a completely new way of producing clothing and
selling it which Miyake has been developing over the past number of years together with textile

1 | The continuous tracks allow every part of the space to be used.
2 | Smaller objects can be placed on trays.

2 |

technician Dai Fujiwara. Long tubes of material are produced on computer-programmed industrial sewing machines from the 1930s and 1940s; the pattern and cut are woven into the material in an enigmatic manner. This allows the customer in the boutique to choose from several different versions that can be "extracted" from the tube of material in an almost miraculous fashion. This means that, in one sense, the design process is moved to the production of the material, but in another sense to the sales area. The A-POC principle can serve as an inspiration for many areas of life and so the two designers, better described as inventors, are constantly looking for contacts to people from related disciplines, such as architects. This makes it less than surprising that the sales outlet and the clothes collection have structural similarities: the intention is to employ design effort in such a way that it creates room for further possibilities.

4 |

3 | A roll of A-POC material is presented on the space-shaping installation.
4 | The pieces of clothing hover in space.

109

GIORGIO ARMANI
cosmetics

EMPORIO ARMANI

MASSIMILIANO FUKSAS AND DORIANA O. MANDRELLI
HONG KONG, CHINA 2001–02

Giorgio Armani is one of the pioneers of consistent architecture branding. In the process he endeavours to adapt the architectural image to suit the different groups targeted by his various lines of products.

Since 1999 Claudio Silvestrin has been developing a reduced look for Armani Boutique that is **based on fine materials** and discrete design. Whereas for the young and less expensive label Emporio Armani, Massimiliano Fuksas and Doriana Mandrelli were, for the first time, commissionied to translate the fashion designer's livelier and more innovative side into architecture. Fuksas and Mandrelli developed an animated interior based on notional movement lines of the public. Curved forms, translucent materials and a lively use of light convey the lightness and relaxed feeling of casual shopping. In the building on Charter Road, at the centre of Hong Kong's business district, all the various Armani lines are included, which, in addition to the fashion lines, means Armani fiori, the bookshop and the cosmetics line. Fuksas and Mandrelli also designed the Armani Café, which has in the meantime become famous. The link running through this design is a gleaming red PVC band that swings with élan through the space, used here as table, there as a DJ stand, at one place as an entrance and at another as bench. A kind of red carpet gone wild.

1 | The entrance area exploits the power of the image.
2 | A red band ensnares the customers ...
3 | ... and whirls around while casually forming counters, tables and seating.

>> 48

2 |

3 |

4 | This dynamism is continued in the sales spaces themselves.
5 | The retail architecture is an almost immaterial formation of glass, bars and light.
6 | The glass staircase.

ROMA

1| 2|

MASSIMILIANO FUKSAS AND DORIANA O. MANDRELLI | ROME, ITALY 2001

Architecture for fashion includes many different typologies ranging from production to sales; much the same applies to the presentation of the designs to the critics and invited guests – the famous shows that are decisive for the success of a collection.

›› 52 **To much the same extent** as the retail outlets these presentations mirror the relationship of the large fashion houses to architecture. On the one hand increasingly exotic locations, such as abattoirs or metro stations, are being chosen to emphasise the presentation as an "event", while on the other the design of the catwalk is increasingly entrusted to professionals, who can be stylists, stage designers or indeed architects. The Roma Fashion Week is centrally positioned with regard to both these trends. On the one hand the location is unusual, EUR (Esposizione universale di Roma) – the exhibition grounds in the southwest of Rome built under Mussolini – is not exactly known for its affinity with fashion. The famous Palazzo dei Ricevimenti e Congressi by Adalberto Libera (1937–1942) with its impressively clear volumes and colonnade recalling the paintings of De Chirico stands there alongside other icons of modern Italian architecture.

FASHION WEEK

ADDRESS:
Palazzo dei Congressi
Piazza John Kennedy 1
Rome, Italy

3 | 4 |

1 | The cubes echo the monumental marble slabs of the wall.
2 + 4 | The rhythm column–void–column is reinterpreted by the fashion photos between the monumental columns.
3 | In designing the foyer, interventions were kept to an absolute minimum.

This was the location for the Roma Fashion Week 2001, an event that is organised annually by the Camera Nazionale della Moda. With their interventions Fuksas and Mandrelli worked on those criteria of the building that most closely reflect the stereotypes of fascist architecture: rhythmical movement, uniformity and a sculptural quality. They strengthened the immanent pathos of this architecture through selecting a powerful red colour that was used because it was (and still is) a symbol for political parties of very different directions, but is nowadays generally associated with the political left. This approach reflects a trend noticeable in fashion since the 1990s to refer increasingly to political themes but without making any unambiguous statements. The search here is more for a general political aura.

LOCATION:
Prada Epicenter
5-2-6 Minami-Aoyama
Minato-ku
Tokyo, Japan
INTERNET:
www.prada.com

PRADA EPICENTER

Two elements are responsible for the enormous effect made by Herzog & de Meuron's building on Omotesando, Tokyo's best-known fashion mile for shopaholics: the public plaza and the striking crystalline form.

1 | The rhombuses are everything in one: display units, windows and a load-bearing frame.
2 | At night the illuminated building has a strong presence in the street space.
3 | So-called snorkels create different moods with sound and images.
4 | The freestanding building has a strikingly impressive form.
5 | The circulation passageways emanate intimacy.

The immediate surroundings are marked by the heterogeneous quality typical of Japanese streets, but only a short distance away you can find one brand-new architectural jewel (with highly fashionable contents) after the other. While the disparate nature of the surroundings meant that the Basel architects were not obliged to pay undue attention to the context, the building had to measure up to the competition on Omotesando, including Dior by SANAA, Louis Vuitton by Jun Aoki and Tod's by Toyo Ito, as well as the Hanae Mori Building by Kenzo Tange and, in the near future, Tadao Ando's Dojunkai Aoyama Apartments.

Jacques Herzog and Pierre de Meuron began to play with the mass of the building like in a board game, moving it from one corner of the lot to the other and finally creating something that represents pure luxury in such surroundings – open space in the form of a public square. At the same time the maximum possible was extracted from the relevant sections of Tokyo's zoning laws, a design approach strikingly reminiscent of the development of the Rockefeller Center in New York in the 1930s. The façades of the building are not only highly transparent in all directions but are also load bearing. This is achieved by the use of a lozenge-shaped steel frame in which large glass panes are set that can be curved, convex or concave, and are generally transparent but occasionally opaque. In the process these recipients of the famous Pritzker Prize closely questioned the relationship between interior, façade and shop window: everything is everything. As the loads are carried by the façades the interior could be freely planned in all three dimensions. The circulation elements in this spatial continuum are formed by accessible steel tubes, in which different moods can be produced by means of images, sounds and light using so-called "snorkels". Shopping here becomes a hallucination, architecture a stimulant.

3 |

4 |

PAUL SMITH

LOCATION:
Paul Smith
Via Manzoni 30, Palazzo Gallarati Scotti
Milan, Italy
INTERNET:
www.paulsmith.co.uk

**In 2001 the second flagship store
of boy wonder Paul Smith
opened in the Palazzo Gallarati Scotti
in Milan's via Manzoni.**

Essentially, the structure of the existing sequence of spaces in the eighteenth-century palazzo, that range from enormously tall to tiny, was retained but with new circulation in the form of stairs and galleries. Elements of the original fittings were visibly patched up, such as the terrazzo flooring in which missing areas were repaired using colourful mosaic. But happily, rather than engaging in a symbiosis, the old and the new cheerfully contradict each other. The individual elements of the fittings have absolutely nothing to do with each other and the more blatant the contrast in the tightest of spaces, the better the result. Here old does not necessary mean elegantly antique but simply worn. A dilapidated workbench that Paul Smith had found on his travels in Italy is used to present bags of the finest quality. Glass display cases can contain lingerie, plastic lobsters or toys. What is suggested here is a circus atmosphere. The spaces are painted in a pink that is a complete exaggeration of the reddish earth tone often used in Italy to paint the outside of houses. It is this "mixture of the precious with the crude" (Deyan Sudjic) that makes the store so like Smith's fashion, for his collections, too, derive their strength from unexpected combinations of completely disparate elements. This is not the first time that Sophie Hicks and Paul Smith have worked together; in 1998 she redesigned Westbourne House, an elegant London townhouse, for Smith, retaining its private character. The contrast between the two flagship stores could hardly be greater. Whereas others may try to build up a recognisable architectural image, Smith lays great emphasis on individualisation. Not surprisingly.

2 |

59 <<

3 |

1+2 | No respect for old age: a wink within old walls.
3 | Hicks and Smith look for the contrast between old and new.

6 |

7 |

4 | A space full of contrasts: large/small, modern/old.
5 | Detail of one of the glass cases.
6 | The original doorway provides a stylish frame.
7 | A discarded workbench is used to show exclusive luggage.

LOUIS VUITTON

Today the box is a building type commonly used throughout the world.

But attempts to integrate it in the urban mesh or to give it something like significance are not always crowned with success.
In this particular case, however, the box makes complete sense, as it is used entirely in the (admittedly already rather dated) context of "architecture parlante". For what, after all, is a suitcase but a kind of box? Content is programme, as it were.
The façade, too, seems to speak in some way, for the lattice of sandstone blocks hangs from above. The stone blocks were first of all fixed on rods in a staggered pattern that left small square openings. It is almost impossible to avoid making an association with rolling shutters that have been let down on all four sides of the building. This is a further variation of a leitmotif found so often in new fashion architecture: semi-transparency or semi-opacity. Kumiko Inui's Vuitton shop in Kochi fits seamlessly into the construction campaign of the company Louis Vuitton Malletier, which, above all in Asia, has devised an expansive branding strategy in which architecture is a principal instrument. The company first used the theme of the box in the Vuitton shop by former boss Jun Aoki, who in Tokyo/Omotesando stacked several glazed boxes on top of each other.

LOCATION:
LouisVuitton Kochi
3-1-1 Harimaya-cya
Kochi-ken
Kochi, Koti, Japan
INTERNET:
www.vuitton.com

1 | A sense of depth is created by overlaying the two facade layers.
2 | The street front.
3 | The display furniture takes up the rhythm of the facade.

LOUIS VUITTON

1 |

LOCATION:
Tod's Omotesando
5-1-15 Jingumae
Shibuya-ku
Tokyo, Japan
INTERNET:
www.tods.com

TOD'S FLAGSHIP STORE

The location is the programme: Omotesando, today Tokyo's most elegant shopping boulevard was originally laid out as the approach to the Meiji Shrine.

Zelkovas, Japanese trees with a mesh of numerous spreading branches, still determine the relaxed atmosphere of the street and inspired Toyo Ito in his design of the flagship store for the label Tod's: 30-cm-thick concrete bands form the load-bearing external skin of the building. These bands run criss-cross to create a net-like or, to put it better, a nest-like structure into which panes of glass are fitted without frames. The apparently random, organic quality of this façade is contrasted with the sharp edges of the trapezoid-shaped building. Like many new buildings for fashion the façade derives its energy from how much of the interior one can see or intimate from outside. But unlike others Ito's building does not emphasise semi-transparency but rather the strong contrast between transparency on the one hand and opacity on the other. A view of the interior is revealed by large areas of glazing but is also arbitrarily sliced by the branching structure of the façade. The shadows cast by the concrete bands give the building additional depth.

The L-shaped building contains seven storeys providing exhibition, sales and office space. In the interior as well the façade bands and the sliced views of the outside dominate the spaces – that also depart from the right angle in plan.

Ito's understanding of architecture has always been influenced by the idea of dismantling the boundaries of space, he fantasises about whirlpools, the flow of the winds and veils of light. For Tod's he has succeeded in achieving this ideal in the form of an airy treetop.

2 |

3 |

4 |

5 |

1 | Oblique views of the world's largest city.
2 | The staircase: the daring format of the windows reveals spectacular views.
3 | The penthouse: the best view from the "treetop" is for the fortunate few.
4 | Sales area: no columns, just display islands.
5 | Spreading branches and intersections: the view from the street shows the relationship between tree and building.

LOCATION:
Dover Street Market
17–18 Dover Street
London, Great Britain

"I would like for DSM to be the place where fashion becomes fascinating" said Rei Kawakubo at the opening of the Dover Street Market in London, a further new shopping concept from the mistress-mind behind the label Comme des Garçons.

She had selected and invited a number of people to join in a common marketing project for avant-garde fashion and art and they all came along: Hedi Slimane, Martin Margiela, Raf Simons, Azzedine Alaïa, Judy Blame, Junya Watanabe and many more. The outcome is a kind of permanent fashion and art fair, a six-storey market hall that offers a changing range of goods. It has, in a sense, become a memorial to the legendary Kensington Market, a platform for young designers that ironically closed down recently.

Each designer invited to present their goods at DSM was allowed to design their own fair or market stall. This led to an enormously rich diversity within a shell that was kept as neutral as possible and where no subdivision of the space was envisaged. Instead of this, small, corrugated metal cabins were erected and large closets and scaffolding define boundaries, while marvellous chandeliers mark centre points. Naturally, such an amount of heterogeneity demands a strong unifying force to avoid losing its balance completely. This is provided by an internal newspaper, DSM Paper, and also by installations by fashion artists, like Stephen Jones, who use the entire space and thus bind it together as a whole. Architecture as art is not to be found in Dover Street Market, instead stage sets and shop window decorations are used to create the "atmosphere of beautiful chaos" that Rei Kawakubo wanted. The jury of the British Fashion Awards was also most impressed and selected Dover Street Market as Shop of the Year 2005.

1 |

2 |

3 |

4 |

1 | The hall itself remains almost completely untouched.
2 | Everything could be altered immediately, or simply vanish.
3+4 | Entirely shabby chic.
5 | Scaffolding and a building container furnish the space.

MONIKA KOWALSKA
NEW YORK, USA 2004

Monika Kowalska
is a designer and
shop owner who regards
herself as a curator.

1 |

Her small shop in SoHo is a cross between a
gallery and an antique shop. Household articles,
decorative art and fashion are combined to create
an ambiance that is highly personal, giving you
the feeling that you are in the designer's living
room. Old photographs are pinned unpretentious-
ly on the walls; a retro sofa and modern chairs
are combined with logs. The objects of the
presentation and the objects presented could not
be more disparate, but the transition is always
flowing. The connecting link in this apparently
chaotic cabinet is the tangible sympathy that
the owner has for the items. And the care with
which she arranges pieces found here and there
to create small poetic groups that occasionally
acquire a faintly surreal quality. This approach
reflects the current anti-architecture trend that
total rejected interventions by interior designers.

Spaces are used in the state in which they are
found, invoking a minimalism that is not im-
posed by any kind of financial constraints but is
entirely aesthetic. And so the vintage principle
is increasingly being applied to the field of
architecture.

"A détacher" — "to be plucked" or "to be taken
away" is the name and programme of both the
collection and the shop.

1 | The mix is the thing: nutcracker and pumice stone.
2 | The atmosphere is unconventional,
complete with motorbike and graffiti.

2 |

A DÉTACHER

LOCATION:
A Détacher
262 Mott Street
New York, USA

THE LONDON

What if... instead of the customers coming to the shop the shop came to the customers?

Barry Laden, owner of the well-known Laden Showroom in East London, which presents and sells clothes by young and still unknown fashion designers, asked himself this very question. By converting a legendary double-decker London bus into a mobile shop with cash desk, fitting rooms, sofas on the first level and a continuous clothes rail upstairs, Laden radically expanded his operating range. Attracting immense publicity the bus toured throughout the UK, making stops at shopping centres, pedestrian zones, modern landmarks such as Selfridges in Birmingham and at epicentres of the fashion business such as the London Fashion Week. The expressed goal of this tour was to recruit a new (young) public for the designs of young designers. This strategy aims at escaping from global uniformity and giving the range of goods on offer in most city centres, which is largely the same everywhere, at least a temporary hint of something special. Clearly, the truism that people must be collected where they are waiting also applies to fashion.

1|

>> **74**

2|

1| The interior has been gently adapted as a sales space.
2| A typical London double-decker bus in a new outfit.

FASHION BUS

Building for Chanel still remains the supreme discipline in the field of fashion architecture, and Tokyo-Ginza is still the ideal location for a kind of Guggenheim of fashion, the largest Chanel boutique in the world.

CHANEL

1 |

The spirit of Coco Chanel, the founder of this fashion house and revolutionary in the world of women's clothing, is consciously invoked by Karl Lagerfeld and still hovers perceptibly over this gigantic business.

Peter Marino had previous experience of dealing with this great name as he carried out the conversion of the hub of this business in rue Cambon in Paris, where he managed to convey something of the atmosphere of the bohemian designer's legendary apartment and studio. The image of this label is strong and direct: striking forms, clear black-and-white contrasts and the powerful lettering dominate (for instance) the ubiquitous cosmetic line. Marino here applies these same characteristics on an architectural scale.

LOCATION:
Chanel
3-5-3 Ginza, Chuo-ku
Tokyo, Japan
INTERNET:
www.chanel.com

1 | The Tweed Garden: a reference to Coco Chanel's favourite cloth.
2 | The name of this exclusive restaurant was Madame's favourite colour.
3 | In the entrance area: the classic perfume Chanel No. 5 is presented as an icon.

5 |

As in most of the new flagship stores the core concern is not shopping alone but also lifestyle and culture. Hence the 10-storey building also contains a concert hall and a restaurant by the name of "Beige Tokyo" – madame's favourite colour – which is run by famous French star chef Alain Ducasse. On the roof, a "Tweed Garden" (the designer's favourite fabric), invites customers to linger. The façade also refers in changing ways to the history of the House of Chanel. A specially appointed art director commands the 700,000 light diodes to generate changing patterns, mostly of tweed. Nor was any extravagance spared in the design of the car parking area at the rear of the building, where white marble and granite fittingly accompany the path of customers from their cars into the three-storey retail area.

4 | Street wear by Chanel.
5 | The interior: restrained colours and the most exclusive materials.

JEAN-PAUL GAULTIER HAUTE COUTURE

ALAIN MOATTI / HENRI RIVIÈRE | PARIS, FRANCE 2001–04

LOCATION:
Jean Paul Gaultier
Rue Saint Martin 325
Paris, France
INTERNET:
www.jeanpaul-gaultier.com

A palais dating from 1912 in the Third Republic style with a more than eventful history – it has been used as a boxing ring, a nightclub and the headquarters of a philanthropical society called "L'Avenir du proletariat" – has been transformed into the headquarters of Jean-Paul Gaultier.

The diversity of its earlier uses is matched by the variety of new functions now housed in the building: fashion showroom, haute couture salon, design studios and ateliers, management offices, press and public relations department as well as the marketing office are all combined under a single roof.

The duo Moatti/Rivière have a holistic approach to architecture, which they view as a "gesamtkunstwerk" perceived with all five senses, and, significantly, their guiding discipline is the experimental cuisine of Ferran Adrià. In this conversion for Jean-Paul Gaultier they worked with strong distorting effects that effectively use the opulence of early twentieth-century architecture but reinterpret it in terms of material. A grand staircase leads to the Salon and the Grand Salle; a 60-metre-long space with two galleries that seems like it was designed with fashion shows in mind. Here black and white form the main colour concept, the surfaces shine, gleam and shimmer in different intensities. The dark, highly polished resin floor is like an unruffled pool of water that reflects light coming from above; during the day through three huge roof lights, at night from monumental crystal chandeliers. The statement is a strong one but that is how it has to be to keep up with the persistently extreme nature of Jean-Paul Gaultier's collections. An aesthetic of the excessive connects these three creative people, all of whom have had experience in the world of film and the stage – surely no mere coincidence.

›› 80

1| A space like a piece of calligraphy.
2| Unusual light-fittings place accents.
3| Clad and alienated: modern stucco ornament.

4 |

4 | Daylight is presented: one of the roof lights in the large hall.
5 | The large hall: everything can happen here.

MANDARINA DUCK

LOCATION:
Mandarina Duck
219, Rue Saint Honoré
Paris, France
INTERNET:
www.mandarinaduck.com

NL ARCHITECTS WITH DROOG DESIGN
PARIS, FRANCE 2000

When designers are allowed to dream. The new shop for Mandarina Duck, an Italian design label for handbags, accessories and (more recently) fashion located in the time-honoured rue Saint Honoré in Paris, was intended to be something never seen before.

First of all the Dutch group Droog Design was commissioned, which then involved NL Architects in the project, another young team from the Netherlands, known above all for their NL Lounge at the Venice Biennale in 2000.

As this was intended to be a "store with no architecture", the walls were treated with great restraint and the interest was focussed on "furniture objects" of very different kinds. Behind the plain glass façade a kind of course was set out leading between various spatial elements, each of them offering material and conceptual surprises and tending more to conceal the goods than display them. A lattice of aluminium rods, in which the bags can be simply fixed, shows their negative imprints on the reverse. What looks like a flying saucer functions as an inverted clothes rack, inside it articles of clothing can be looked at in peace and quiet. A curtain made of metal chains surrounds the display of handbags. The most dynamic element is a rotating spiral staircase – a kind of cross between a lift and a revolving door. Unusual methods of fixing provide repeated surprises: simple horizontally stretched rubber bands hold handbags, while vacuum-packed articles of clothing seem to hover in the air. But what really takes the biscuit is the design of the fitting rooms, a kind of steppe landscape made of fibreglass rods as tall as a human being, which define small clearings where customers are intended not to picnic but to try on new clothes. The entire shop gives the impression that the designers had an enormous amount of fun here – so, too, do the customers.

1 | Space is diffusely separated using a
kind of chain mail shirt.
2 + 3 | The fitting-out is oriented towards
customers with a sense of fun.
4 | The systems and materials are flexible.

4 |

PRADA EPICENTER

OMA OFFICE FOR METROPOLITAN ARCHITECTURE
LOS ANGELES, CALIFORNIA, USA 2004

LOCATION:
Prada Epicenter
343 North Rodeo Drive
Los Angeles, CA, USA
INTERNET:
www.prada.com

1 | The mirrored grotto under the staircase.
2 | The large staircase dominates the space.
3 | 343 Rodeo Drive – an epicentere of the fashion world.

Prada and OMA, OMA and Prada, to date one of the most successful examples of collaboration between architecture and fashion.

Both labels like to stay a little ahead of the zeitgeist and, thanks to their collaboration, they have even been able to increase the gap between themselves and their rivals. The success of this combination is certainly based on a similar kind of perfectionism and a comparable theatricality in the design of textiles on the one hand and buildings on the other. Yet there are clearly differences that lend the presentation as a whole a certain excitement. Whereas Miuccia Prada often expressly includes historical models in her collections, Rem Koolhaas – spiritus rector of OMA – and Ole Scheeren refuse to work in any discernible way with historic images. Often indeed it is a kind of architectural reversal that forms the guiding idea behind their design – as in the Prada Epicenter in Los Angeles.

The fashion earthquake suggested by the name has its centre at 343 Rodeo Drive. The building negates the classic façade and the usual controlled entrance situation. It is open to the street along its entire length and is only climatically protected and closed at night by an aluminium grille. As in the already legendary flagship store in New York the interior becomes a stage on which customers can see and be seen. A double flight staircase – the "hill" – fills the space which is both a means of circulation and a presentation area for fashion and the fashion-conscious: the Spanish Steps, or the grand staircase in Garnier's Paris Opera, made for Los Angeles. The various pieces of clothing lie casually on podia or directly on the steps. The staircase forms the centre. This truly baroque concept is completed by the mirrored grotto underneath the staircase with display cases for handbags and shoes. The staircase "hill" leads to a projecting bay window at first-floor level that dominates the façade externally. Light floods through the walls of this box that is made of "sponge", a porous material developed especially for Prada. Prada Los Angeles is far more open than it might seem at first glance.

4+5 | The porous wall material creates a special atmosphere.
5 | The steps are both a display area and a means of circulation.

MAISON HERMÈS

The Maison Hermès in Ginza was to be like a "magic lantern" but of a robust kind that can survive the next earthquake.

LOCATION:
Maison, Hermès
4-1 Ginza 5-chome, Chuo-ku
Tokyo, Japan
INTERNET:
www.hermes.com

On a long and narrow site an elegant structure made of specially developed glass blocks was erected that adds a further facet to the currently popular theme of semi-transparency. Transparent blocks set at eye level allow a view of the interior and the rich colours of the Hermès products. Veiling and revealing has recently become one of the principal themes of "architecture for fashion". At night the 11-storey building does indeed shine like a traditional Japanese lantern. Through its homogeneity it can assert itself in the visual chaos of advertising lights and traffic that constitutes modern Tokyo.

Renzo Piano has not overlooked the aspect of urban planning. At the centre of his building, which lies on an extremely narrow side street, he inserted a tiny square that leads to an underground railway two storeys below. Those familiar with the role played by the underground railway in the world's largest metropolis will realise how clever this move was. Not only does it increase public awareness of the building and the number of people who visit it, but department stores or shopping centres connected to an underground station, which are known as "depato", have developed in Tokyo into new public sub-centres that form a focus of consumption, communication and, increasingly, of culture also.

This building reflects the multi-functional quality of a "depato" (by now an almost traditional urban element) on a smaller scale. In addition to the retail area it includes exhibition spaces, a leather workshop, a small cinema and a museum devoted to the history of Hermès. Furthermore this tower of light forms a successful counterpart to the Sony Building by Ashihara Yoshinobu (1966) that has similar proportions. A flexible "spine" made of shock absorbers enables the new structure to deal with the movement caused by an earthquake. The Ove Arup partnership was responsible for this ingenious construction. A similar principle has been used up to the present day in traditional Japanese temple architecture. A combination of tradition and wit has always been one of the trademarks of Hermès products, now the same can be also be said of the company's architecture.

1 | The Maison Hermès as a kind of magic lantern.

2 + 3 | The glass brick
façade glows in the dark.

CAROL CHRISTIAN POELL | MILAN, ITALY 2003

MAINSTREAM

The work of Carol Christian Poell is a unique hybrid of fashion, art, social involvement, actionism and performance. The collection forms the centre point and is embedded in unusual presentations that in turn lead to extraordinary documentations in the form of photographs or videos. But while expanding the concept of fashion Poell at the same time succeeds in deepening it. No fabric, no seam, no material or pleat remains unquestioned. The materials manipulated with technologies specially developed for the purpose move into surreal realms such as that of transparent horse leather. The absolute consistency with which this fashion artist analyses the individual elements in detail, distorts and then re-assembles them to form a collection does not proclaim their radicalism. The subversive quality is often only revealed at a second or third glance.

His fashion shows are accordingly irritating. Whether it be an abattoir, dog pound or the FLAG tower Poell always chooses threatening places that heighten the fragility of the clothes and the models and make explicit a sense of being exposed through beauty. In his most extreme presentation to date, Mainstream-Downstream, in June 2003 he let the models wearing the clothes from his

**"There with fantastic garlands did she come
Of crow-flowers, nettles, daisies, and long purples"**

DOWNSTREAM

summer collection 2004 drift motionless in the waters of Naviglio Grande in Milan. The macabre character of this presentation and the associations with Shakespeare's Ophelia are clear. The distortion through a denser medium and the reduced pull of gravity emphasise his design strategy. The title Mainstream-Downstream can also refer to the Naviglio itself. This canal completed in the fourteenth century was the first of a branching system of waterways and until 1979 remained an important public transport route in the city. With his action Poell restored an awareness of this area of water as a public space.

"Her clothes spread wide,
And, mermaid-like, awhile they bore her up"
William Shakespeare, Hamlet, Act IV, Scene VII

Fashion manufacturing is a dirty business; production is often connected with social hardship and unsatisfactory ecological conditions.

As a result of the progress of globalisation production has disappeared from sight – precisely what goes on in southeast Asia or in South America is lost in the vastness of the global market with its labyrinthine company structures and middlemen. But one thing is certain. It is not always the manufacturers of cheap clothing that offer the worst working conditions, a number of luxury labels increase their profit margins at the expense of unprotected workers, generally women who are not organised in unions and are the real fashion victims. Yet all the same there is also a growing awareness among both manufacturers and consumers and the demand for politically and ecologically correct labels is growing.

Architecture always includes the spatial translation of social structures and therefore intelligent measures can help to improve the position of workers in the clothing industry. The project "23 de Enero" for Caracas, Venezuela by Katharina Rohde shows how, using focussed minimal interventions, an existing super-block (23 de Enero) could be transformed from a purely residential building into a workplace for the female residents, most of whom are unemployed. The women are given a sewing machine, they do the work in their own living rooms. But in contrast to other home-working models that, particularly in the clothing business, are often carried out under unacceptable conditions, in this project childcare facilities and training are provided and links are built up among the women. A magazine keeps the flow of information going. The actual built intervention would concentrate on the roof of the mega-block, where, using restricted material means, a forum for training, fashion shows and other cultural events is to be erected. The visualisation of this intervention shows that cutting edge and social awareness are not contradictory but, in the best of cases, can actually complement each other.

1 | The intention is that all the people in the blocks should profit from the intervention.
2 | The level of organisation is intended as a protection against exploitation.
3 | The women can work in their own living rooms.
4 | Fashion production is always also political.
5 | There is room on the roof of the block for work training and events.
6 | Analysis of the population density.

"23 DE ENERO"

5 |

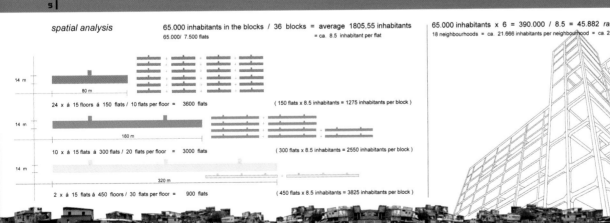

spatial analysis   65.000 inhabitants in the blocks / 36 blocks = average 1805,55 inhabitants

65.000/ 7.500 flats   = ca. 8.5 inhabitant per flat

65.000 inhabitants x 6 = 390.000 / 8.5 = 45.882 *ranchos*

18 neighbourhoods = ca. 21.666 inhabitants per neighbourhood = ca. 2549 *ranchos* per neighbourhood

14 m

80 m

24 x á 15 floors á 150 flats / 10 flats per floor =   3600 flats   (150 flats x 8.5 inhabitants = 1275 inhabitants per block)

14 m

160 m

10 x 15 flats á 300 flats / 20 flats per floor =   3000 flats   (300 flats x 8.5 inhabitants = 2550 inhabitants per block)

14 m

320 m

2 x 15 flats á 450 floors / 30 flats per floor =   900 flats   (450 flats x 8.5 inhabitants = 3825 inhabitants per block)

6 |

1|

JUST CAVALLI

The aim was to make Roberto Cavalli's shop in Milan every bit as startling as his designs.

2|

And indeed this conversion is bursting with eye-catchers and special features of every kind. This approach may go against the advice of every shop-fitting consultant as well as infringing on the notion of good taste embodied in the famous dictate "less is more", but it is certainly extremely witty. As Alessandro Pedretti, the partner of Italo Rota, explains: "It's a wonderland, a surprising place that combines natural elements with space-age overtones."

One highpoint of this intentionally over-the-top presentation is the giant aquarium separating the restaurant lounge from the shopping area. The lift is also striking: it is a padded white cell lined with fur and faux leather resembling part of the set for an Austin Powers film. To while away the time spent travelling between floors champagne is offered and videos of the most recent Cavalli shows can be viewed on a monitor. Those for whom even this is too tedious can admire their reflection in the walls to the red-carpeted spiral stairs: "absolutely fabulous!"

1 + 2 | View of the sales area.

LOCATION:
Just Cavalli
Via Spiga 42
Milan, Italy
INTERNET:
www.robertocavalli.net

3 |

3 | The aquarium as a screen.
4 | Everything here revolves around the individual ego.

The first impression made by the new Dior flagship store in Tokyo is one of elegance.

The white façade has the silky transparency of chiffon, an effect achieved by the use of slightly curved, printed polyethylene panels that are placed behind an outer layer of glass and transform the full transparency of the external skin into opacity of different degrees. The aluminium bands holding these "folds" at rhythmical intervals mark the floor levels as well as the spaces for mechanical services. Here, once more, the "principle of clothing" has been applied to the architecture, but the reference is to traditional Japanese clothing, which follows very different principles to European costume. The stiff folds, the dominance of white and the closed outline are reminiscent of the traditional Japanese wedding kimono. Compared to European garments traditional Japanese clothing is very static; rather than emphasising the movement of draped fabric Japanese costume design concentrates on precision and an unchanging quality. In exactly the same way as a Japanese kimono the façade by Kazuyo Sejima and Ryue Nishizawa conveys a sense of timelessness in one of the ritziest locations in Tokyo, a city characterised by a notorious rate of change.

The interior fittings for the various Dior lines were designed by Peter Marino and Architecture & Associés (ladies' fashions on the first two floors), and by Hedi Slimane (men's fashions on the lower ground floor). Here the use of lacquered surfaces, mirrors and silk to produce an opulent "French" interior creates a considerable contrast to the plain exterior.

In addition to the various Dior lines, the building also houses a multi-functional events space and a roof garden. The latest technology has arrived in the Dior empire: the fitting rooms no longer have mirrors, instead cameras offer simultaneous views of all four well-dressed sides.

LOCATION:
Dior
5-9-11 Jingumae, Shibuy-ku
Tokyo, Japan
INTERNET:
www.fashion.dior.com

1 | The tower has a strikingly restrained elegance.
2 | No harsh tones at Dior Tokyo.

Dior Omotesando

MZ WALLACE

1|

ANNABELLE SELLDORF | NEW YORK, USA 2001

Annabelle Selldorf's commissions are generally small in scale but of the finest quality. She has acquired a reputation for carrying out some of the most subtle conversions of historic building fabric in New York, Zurich and Venice, including a striking number of private collections, galleries and smaller museums.

LOCATION:
MZ Wallace
93 Corby Street
New York, USA
INTERNET:
www.mzwallace.com

1 + 2 | The raw character of the space is continued in the fittings. The armchairs are by Franz West.

2 |

In the shop for MZ Wallace, designer of highly desirable handbags, Selldorf combines New York understatement with European art in a virtuoso manner. Her approach involves only minimal interventions. The spatial envelope was left the way it was found, the exposed brick walls were painted white, the concrete floor left untreated, the pipes running just below the ceiling were not concealed. The fittings were also reduced to a minimum. A number of bags hang directly from brass hooks, the shelves are fixed to normal wall brackets. Traditional lamps with simple glass shades are arranged in rows parallel to the edges of the space (the way fluorescent tubes are generally mounted). This mixture of bareness and old-fashioned charm is echoed in an especially subtle way by Viennese artist Franz West's seating furniture. In these pieces, too, the use of material is reduced to a minimum yet they still emanate a feeling of home, perhaps even a hint of gemütlichkeit.

SKYLAB DESIGN GROUP
DENVER, COLORADO, USA 2005

On the occasion of the twentieth anniversary of the Air Jordan brand, produced by the world-famous Nike label, the office of Skylab Designs in Portland Oregon, alias Jeffery S. Kovel, was commissioned to convert a warehouse into a temporary event space with showrooms and a VIP lounge that was also to serve as the location for the launch of special anniversary shoe, Air Jordan XX.

Jeffrey Kovel, a specialist for entertainment architecture, was given the prototype of the shoe and began to develop a spatial concept from it. However it was not the shoe but rather Michael "Air" Jordan, the legendary New York basketball player who has had an advertising contract with Nike for two decades, that formed the centre point of the presentation. Today the Jordan line includes clothing as well as the original sneakers.

The entrance is already dominated by an oversized photograph of "His Airness" that presents the impressive full span of his outstretched arms. Inside is full of glamour and glitter, a tunnel with porthole display cases leads to the lounge in which seating landscapes and computers offer an invitation to hang out in style. Skylab has created an appropriate environment for the virtual parallel universe. The collaboration between Skylab and Nike also includes the Nike Studio @ 255 in downtown Manhattan, where the most advanced lines of this label are presented. Since the 1990s Nike has established itself worldwide in urban systems, above all through the erection of Niketowns that have occasionally been the cause of heated debates.

>> 108

LOCATION:
Jordan XXperience
1825 Blake Street
Denver, CO USA

JORDAN XXPERIENCE

3

2 + 3 | "His Airness" rules here.

4 | The stages of a career.
5 | There is a Spaceship Enterprise feeling here.
6 | The lounge area: no entry without the right sneakers.
7 | Everything revolves around the sports shoe.

LOCATION:
Elie Tahari Showroom
417 West Broadway
New York, USA
INTERNET:
www.elietahari.com

1

Elie Tahari Showroom

The task was to convert a leftover space, windowless and crudely interrupted by a beam, into the showrooms of Elie Tahari. Architect and dancer Gisela Stromeyer took on this challenge by using cloth to transform this space for clothes into a transparent white tent.

White sails with the thickness and elasticity of a swimsuit are stretched in a strict choreography through the space, attached to hooks and weights on the walls and floor. The curving forms of the sails create a flighty physical effect; the lengths of fabric seem frozen in motion. The way in which the tensioned material creates vaults of a very different kind has something eminently architectural about it, even though the entire cladding can be taken down and washed when necessary. Concealed lighting helps one forget the dreary concrete shell enclosing the dream tent.

In a sense working architecturally with fabrics is in Gisela Stromeyer's blood, as her father Peter Stromeyer, a third-generation German tentmaker, worked with Frei Otto on the concept for the "Tanzbrunnen" in Cologne and on the German Pavilion in Montreal. His daughter uses her interior sails to set lofts, dance stages, shops and swimming pools in motion.

1 | The displayed articles of clothing connect with the fittings of the space.
2 | Weights hold the textile sails in place.
3 | The structure's functional flexibility is part of the aesthetic concept.
4 | A central pier is clad with sails.

5 |

PLAN:
CENTER COLUMN:

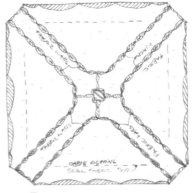

6 |

PLAN: FABRIC CEILING

...frozen in motion.

7 |

ELEVATION: FABRIC CEILING

5-8 | The artist's preliminary drawings show the vaulted spatial structure.

9 | Stromeyer is also a dancer, movement in space is her theme.

8 |

9 |

It is certainly an honour when a shop is used as a setting in the cult TV series of all fashionistas on this planet (and probably on a few other ones also).

In episode 62 of the fourth series of "Sex and the City" Carrie and Miranda go shopping in the Kerquelen Shoe Store, which since then has been a fixed stop on the list of places to visit in New York for "Sex and the City" addicts.

Designing high-flying shopping spaces for extreme fashion makers was not a novelty for the Zurich duo Isa Stuerm and Urs Wolf, they had, after all, worked for Issey Miyake and Yohji Yamamoto in Zurich. But in New York the objective was to display an international selection of shoes that due to their often sculptural qualities and the banal fact that they are tried on directly in the sales space demanded a rather different approach. The long, narrow plan was articulated using undulating walls in a practical application of the laws of flow theory (according to which the speed of flow increases at narrower points) to New York shoe fetishists. In contrast the broader areas and bays offer seats made of colourful, filled leather balls to recline in and to try on shoes. Slender piers define the route like the rods marking the gates in a slalom race. A ceiling mirror sprayed on by hand reveals a view of an "artificial skyscape". A mirrored wall at the back of the space opens what looks like a "passageway continuing through the whole block to East Broadway", according to the architects. Both illusions, the real mirror and the painted ceiling, engage each other, awakening faint memories of arcades in London or Paris, the lost paradise of shopping.

LOCATION:
Kerquelen
430 West Broadway
New York, USA
INTERNET:
www.sabinedesign.com

1|

KERQUELEN SHOE STORE II

1 | Silver rods articulate the space.
2 | The large surfaces balance the small scale of the objects.
3 | The shoe as a unique item ...
4 | ... and as one of a series.

5 | The ceiling is consciously displayed.
6 | View of the sales space.

The new shop of the Dutch designer duo, Viktor & Rolf, looks like some kind of joke. The whole space is inverted, even the entrance door with the sign and the doormat.

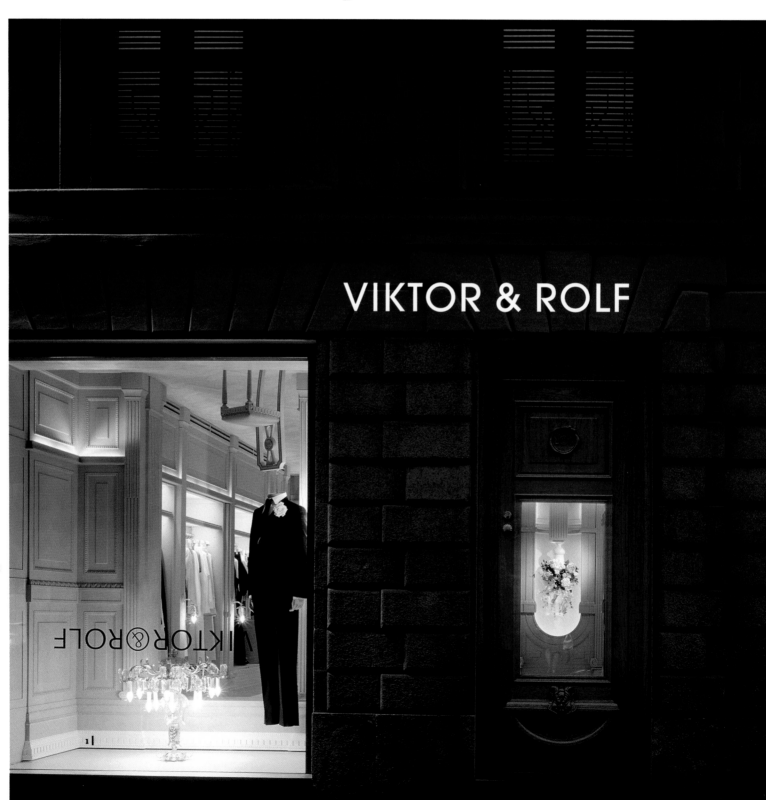

LOCATION:
Viktor & Rolf
Via Sant' Andrea 14
Milan, Italy
INTERNET:
www.viktor-rolf.com

If it were simply a modern box or a neo-modern bubble then it might not attract any further attention, for this very reason the architects decided, after making lengthy studies of images turned upside down, to design a neoclassical interior. "People have to be familiar with the visual vocabulary, so everyone recognises things as being inverted," Tettero explains. "If you just turn a plain rectangle upside down, nothing happens." The consistency with which the architect and the interior designer create the illusion of standing on one's head and seemingly suspend the laws of gravity is truly impressive. From the wooden parquet on the ceiling to the chandelier growing out of the floor and the packed items on the shelves everything has been thought of. Only a few details take account of the real situation such as the seating cushions lying in the arches of the arcade, the cash desk and the toilets.

This charade refers to old traditions. Crazy proportions, deceptive perspectives, cabinets of mirrors – architectural history can cite any number of strange buildings that intend to irritate as a source of amusement. Yet dream worlds of this kind no longer exist in our globalised shopping universe, only in children's books like the works of Lewis Carroll and in the heads of Viktor Horsting and Rolf Snoeren. Turning the space upside down was one of the clients' initial requirements. Viktor & Rolf are regarded as intelligent critics of the fashion machinery. In their collections they turn the underlying circumstances of fashion, and the way it is presented and sold upside down, so to speak. One time a single model presented the entire collection, which she wore as a series of layers. In the winter collection for 2005 objects such as pillows and blankets were included. "We draw our inspiration from the classics and also from clichés. But we make the details larger than they actually should be or we multiply them, placing them over each other several times," says Rolf, defining their design strategy.

3 |

1 | Consistent, even outside: the lettering is also upside down.
2 | An upside down world is one of these designers' favourite themes.
3 | The arch offers somewhere to sit.
4 + 5 | A wonderland for the fashion conscious.

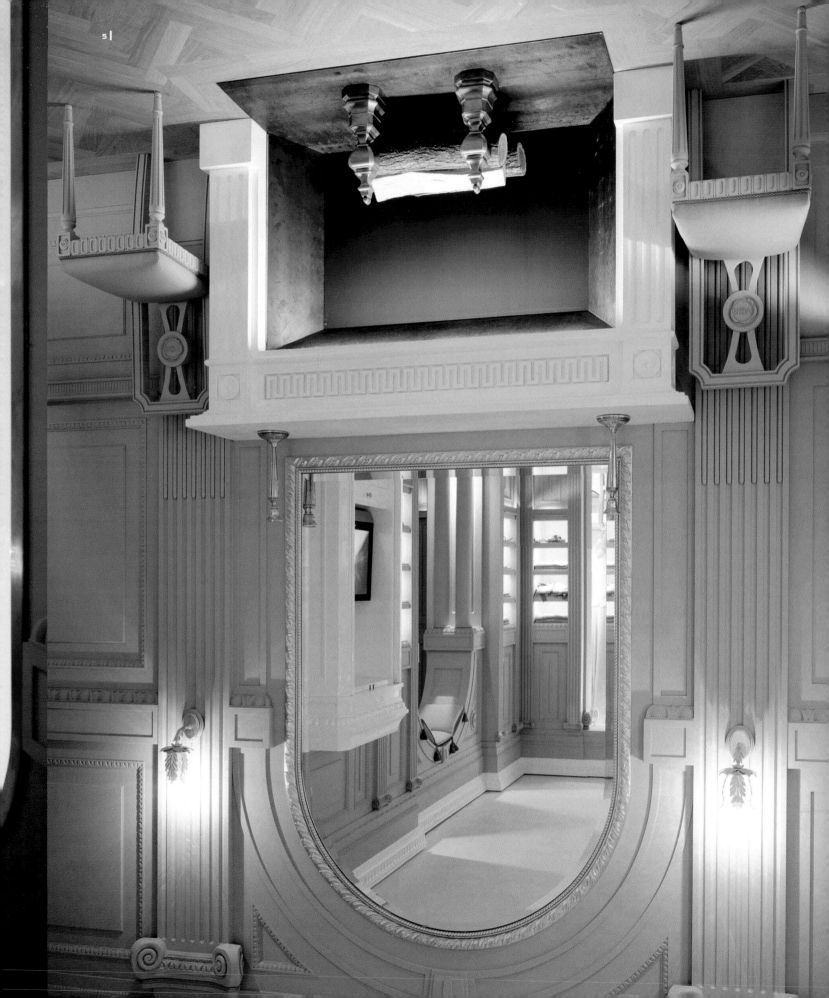

PLUG IN – MOBILE RETAIL CONCEPT

"The provocation of the random and the unpredictable is our strategy for producing spatial and functional agendas for architecture. We work at divining those factors which lead beyond pure functionality — it is how we see the essence of architecture."

This is how Marie-Therese Harnoncourt and Ernst J. Fuchs introduce their design strategy. In this particular case the unpredictable is the location: "plug-in – mobile retail concept" is a transportable boutique that can be set up anywhere. It was made for the Viennese "Büro unit-f Büro für Mode", an interface between designers, the public and industry. The internal dimensions of the smallest conventional transit container defined the spatial boundaries of the four different elements. They were stacked inside each other for transport, much like the Russian Babushka nesting dolls, and set up on site as required. The variety of ways of combining the different elements is increased by the various placements of clothing. This is where the structural relationship to fashion lies, for is it not combination that makes fashion so diverse and so individual?

Naturally, this plug-in concept recalls the "Plug-in City" of the Archigram group from the 1960s, but the undoubted quality of this shop concept is that it could, in fact, function.

INTERNET:
www.unit-f.at

ADDITIVES

1 |

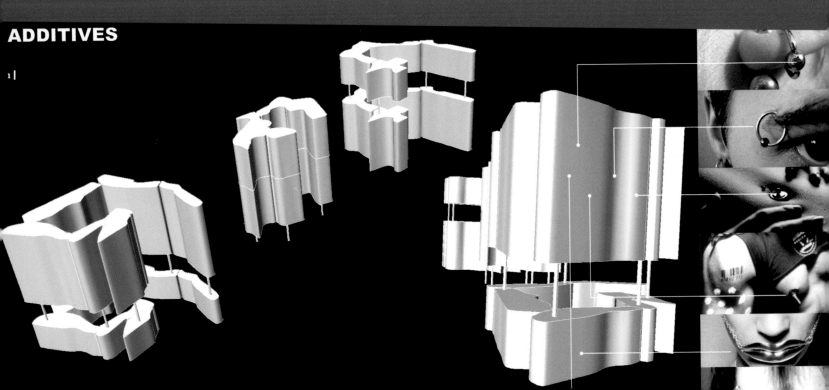

3 |

2 |

1 | The concept consists of four main elements that are used for different forms of presentation.

2 + 3 | The elements can be differently equipped.

"... and I walk down the street and I bop to the beat with Lee on my legs and adidas on my feet..."

Run DMC, My adidas

1 |

1 | At night the clear forms attract the attention of people driving past.
2 | The materials used are reminiscent of a sports hall.

At a performance by the rap band Run DMC in New York hundreds of young people waved with their cheap boots (hitherto regarded as something unspectacular) in time to the song My adidas. This was the start of the legendary revamp of the successful German sports shoe brand. Or so the legend goes. Then followed designs by the Japanese star designer Yohji Yamamoto and the rest is history...

In Herzogenaurach, where the adidas company has been based since it was founded in 1924, a need was perceived to give this success an architectural expression. An urban planning competition for the entire site — a former barracks and a golf course — was won by Marc Angélil and Anna Klingmann. The buildings erected to date include the casino by Kauffmann and Theilig and the adidas factory outlet, while the adi dassler brand centre designed by querkraft architects from Vienna will be completed in 2006. The outlet is a kind of sales warehouse intended to underscore the myth of these young, dynamic sports shoes.

From the distance the new outlet building by Tobias Wulf, Kai Bierich and Alexander Vohl from Stuttgart looks like a white, sleek ship, with a tower as a central orientation point. Access is through an underground garage, as you can reach this outlet only by car. From there you enter the complex by first scurrying across a forecourt with an arena that is used for film presentations and, of course, for skateboarding. Inside the issue is not merely shopping in the traditional sense but enjoying the entire experience. Loudspeakers and monitors hanging from the ceiling inform about sporting events. There is a coffee bar as well as shoe and sport fashions on several levels. The urban, sportive connotations of the sneakers are reflected in the materials used: exposed concrete, industrial glazing and untreated screed. This is how the street chic of the three-stripe label is translated into architecture.

2 |

adidas FACTORY OUTLET

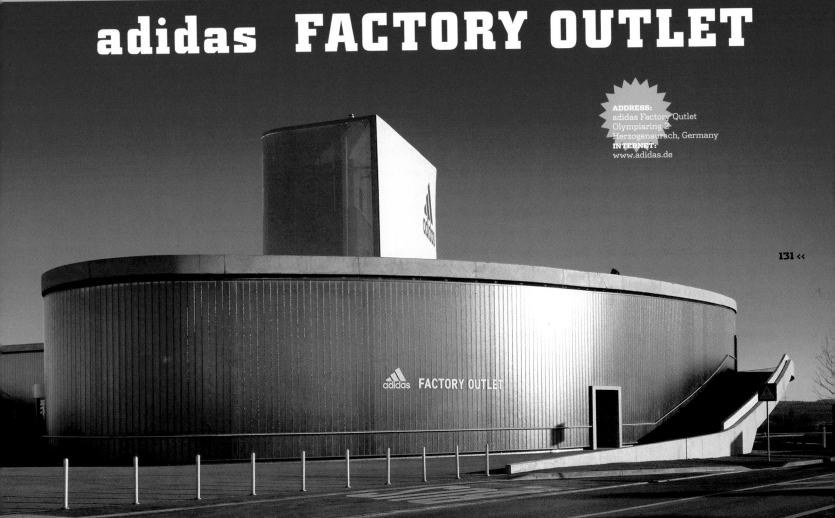

ADDRESS:
adidas Factory Outlet
Olympiaring 2
Herzogenaurach, Germany
INTERNET:
www.adidas.de

3 | A ramp leads into the sales space.
4 | The coffee bar.

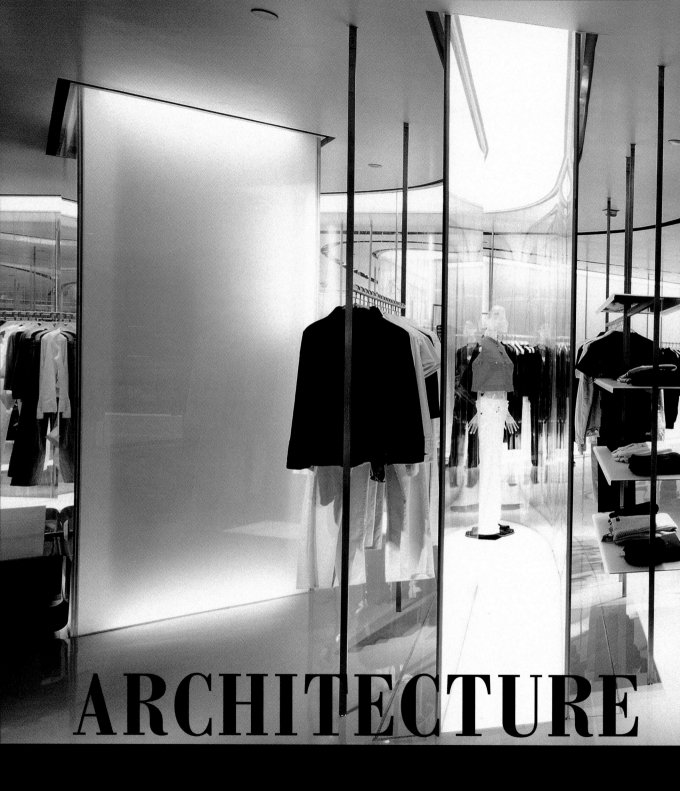

ARCHITECTURE

"Fashion is fleeting, style never changes. Chanel is style."

COCO CHANEL

AND FASHION

Fashion and modern architecture have a closely interwoven common history; architecture and clothing, if we agree with Gottfried Semper, have an even older, primeval relationship. For Semper every wall originally derived from textile techniques and was further developed through one or several "changes of material". In architecture of all periods this original "principle of clothing", as he calls it in his main work "Der Stil" (1860), repeatedly makes its way to the surface.

Around 1900 the relationship between architecture and fashion entered a critical phase; from this time onwards the clothing theory was expanded by the notion of fashion's pioneering role for architecture. There followed a hype of textile metaphors in architecture and an even more extreme one in the field of architectural theory, which discovered in the plainness, practicality, uniformity and, not least of all, the unchanging quality of a simple dark men's suit – as established by the English dandy Beau Brummel about a century previously – the model for modern architecture. Viennese architect Otto Wagner was one of those who examined the relationship between architecture and fashion, not only in theory but also in practice. "The pictures of style just evoked logically allow us to perceive the close and hitherto ignored relationship between taste, fashion and style. Even a slight gift of observation must awaken in us the conviction that outward appearance – man's clothing in its form, colour and accessories – is fully consistent with each period's artistic viewpoints and creations and cannot even be imagined otherwise. [...] A man in a modern travelling suit, for example, fits in very well with the waiting room of a train station, with sleeping cars, with all our vehicles; yet would we not stare if we were to see someone dressed in clothing from the Louis XV period using such things? This extraordinary sensitivity of the public with regard to fashion, on the one hand, and this indifference, even dullness, concerning artistic works, on the other hand, find their explanation in the following. First of all, fashion is more obvious, easier to understand and to influence, a precursor of style, whereas style itself represents something more difficult to influence, a rigid and refined taste whose critique demands concentration and understanding." (Otto Wagner, "Modern Architecture", 1896)

For Adolf Loos, a contemporary of Wagner and himself a dandy in the truest sense of the term, ladies' fashion was the expression of everything in this world that was in bad taste. In an article entitled 'Damenmode' (Ladies' Fashion) published in 1898 in the Neue Freie Presse he wrote: "Ladies' fashion! What a horrible chapter of our cultural history, laying bare mankind's secret lusts. Reading its pages, one shudders to one's very soul at dreadful perversions and unbelievable vices; one can hear the whimpering of abused children, the shrieks of maltreated

women, the ear-splitting screams of tortured people, the wailing of victims burning at the stake. Whips crack, and the air is filled with the smell of roasting human flesh. 'La bête humaine...'" Loos' horror of female accoutrements suggests that he did not regard ladies' fashion as a suitable model for architecture but, on the contrary, saw it as an example of all that was wrong in design. For safety's sake Loos liked to choose his wives' clothing himself. The development of modern architecture therefore is indebted to both ladies' and men's fashion for important impulses: it was as intensely disgusted by the former as it was attracted by the latter. But change also entered the world of ladies' fashion. Various movements to reform women's

Issey Miyake,
'Minaret',
Spring/Summer 1995

clothing in which renowned architects such as Josef Hoffmann, Peter Behrens and Henry van de Velde took part were ignored by the public until, in the 1920s, Coco Chanel took pity and invented the equivalent of the dinner jacket for women: the suit and the little black dress.

"Fashion is a form of ugliness so intolerable that we have to alter it every six months." Oscar Wilde

But in another respect fashion served architecture theory as a buffer. Architecture neither wanted to nor could imitate the rapid changes of fashion, here most people tended to agree with Frank Lloyd Wright (see his motto at the beginning of this essay). When architecture of the transitional period between the late nineteenth and early twentieth century suggested the dark suit as a model, it was aiming at precisely those qualities that made this kind of suit a "classic" that undergoes only slight variations. There are a number of good reasons to view architecture as a medium that for the most part distances itself from the whims of fashion. Val K. Warke wrote in 1994: "The capacity for an object-type (a piece of costume, jewellery, a pair of shoes, a car, an office building) to undergo formal change as a result of a fashion shift is related directly to the size of the object, its cost, the time lag between its initial design and the final act of its consumption, the total amount of production occurring within a specific market, and the time interval between the production of the object and the dispersal of its carefully delimited representations throughout the market." It is exactly this "seriousness" in the production of architecture that so strongly attracts fashion makers, as many of them battle against taunts about the triviality of fashion and yearn for the intellectual quality of architecture. "Here was a domain that simply swirled with theories, that had a tradition of debate leading back to Socrates and Plato, and that was confident enough to mantle itself in bog words like 'modern', and even 'post-modern'", wrote Kenneth Fraser in his critique of the ex-hibition 'Intimate Architecture: Contemporary Clothing Design' in the Hayden Gallery in Cambridge, Massachusetts in 1982. In fact at first glance fashion and architecture have very differ-ent half-lives, for even though occasionally a building may be planned and built in the record period of a single year, in the same length of time at least two haute couture collections can be presented, not to mention the weekly turnaround in the fashions offered at Zara and H&M. But this is not true in all cases. In fashion, too, there are longer-lasting trends and cer-tain designers develop personal styles that characterise their entire life's work. Therefore it can safely be said: fashion is not always short-lived nor architecture always long-lasting. Take

Lucy Orta, 'Refuge Wear, Intervention London East End 1998', 2001

Lucy Orta, 'Nexus Architecture x 50, Nexus Intervention in the City Space Köln', Cologne, Germany 2001

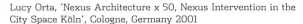

Hans Kollhoff and Helga Timmermann, 'Dressater', Fashion Show at the Hamburger Bahnhof, Berlin, Germany 1988

for example Madame Coco's famous little black dress from 1926, is it not still as elegant and seductive today as it ever was? Could we not, without hesitating, place Audrey Hepburn in a Givenchy dress on the steps of many buildings from the 1960s, and be certain which would look better? Don't many buildings from the 1980s look more dated than a trouser suit by Jil Sander or Gabriele Strenesse? While accepting this one could still argue that, in terms of material, architecture is always more perm-anent than clothing. But even this is not inevitably the case; Ötzi's clothing has survived whereas his hut has not. An extreme case admittedly, but one that shows there is no fixed relationship between fashion and clothing, just a number of changing ones. What does exist, however, is the association in people's minds of fashion with transience and architecture with permanence. But in the last two decades evaluations in these categories have started to change. Whereas for the early, middle and late twentieth century fashion was still associated

with the spectre of vicissitude, today the speed with which fashion can adapt to new circumstances often fascinates architects. "If architecture is still heavy, slow and expensive" demanded Kayus Varnelis in 2001, "it will have to become faster, cheaper, and more responsive. If architecture, still dominated by a 'couture' culture of avant-gardist elitism, is to survive, it must realise that 'haute couture' is doomed, or at the very least, can be only one fashion system among many. Instead, architecture will have to find out how to take advantage of a society in which difference is no longer something only for the very rich, but is now for everyone."

One trigger was the theory of architecture itself. A seminar held by Val K. Warke at Cornell University in 1987 introduced

the theme into a serious theoretical debate, in 1991 there followed the conference 'Architecture: In Fashion', at which the relationship between fashion and architecture was systematically examined for the first time. This introduced a change of paradigms, the assumed superiority of architecture was increasingly questioned by intellectual architects, the marketing strategies surrounding architecture were equated with those of the "fashion sausage machine" thus invalidating architecture's claim to moral superiority. As the French poststructuralist philosophy of Michel Foucault and Jacques Derrida grew more widely known and influential the dominant hier-archies of categories were basically turned upside down, much to the profit of the area of fashion, often an easy target for ridicule. Additionally, the gender debate questioned the often uncriti-cally accepted association of fashion with the female and architecture with the male. But it was not only architecture that chose fashion as its model. The boundaries between pure art, performance and fashion generally became more permeable.

In the 1990s fashion designers and artists explored the borders between fashion and architecture in increasingly radical ways. Astonishingly it was the essentially architectural criteria of construction and function that represented the greatest challenge. If it can stand without a human body does a piece of clothing become a shell, like Issey Miyake's 'Minaret' from the Spring/Summer collection 1995? Or if it offers two persons shelter, like Lucy Orta's 'Refuge Wear, Collective Survival Sac 2 persons' from 1994? What is the effect of connecting several persons through pieces of clothing like the 'Nexus Architecture x 50, Nexus Intervention in the City Space' in Cologne 2001 also by Lucy Orta; is this perhaps a kind of urbanism? For a generation of Japanese designers of the post-war era in particular these radical questions grew increasingly urgent. "Architecture of the skin" was what Yohji Yamamoto called his models and designed a 'Secret Dress' for his Spring/Summer collection 1999 in which the crinoline could also be used as storage space. Architectural metaphors also play a major role in the designers' perception of themselves: the Tunisian Azzedine Alaïa, who converted from a sculptor to a fashion designer, describes himself as a 'bâtisseur' or builder. Hussein Chalayan presented clothes that become tables and chairs under the title 'Afterwords' in Autumn/Winter 2000/01, the perfect environment for modern nomads. Moreover fashion has expanded into urban space: the defilées are increasingly often held in the most unlikely places such as metro stations, abattoirs and street corners. Carol Christian Poell's defilées are the most radical, to date he has used a prison and the Navaglio Grande in Milan as settings to present his work. Fashion has expanded from the niches of haute couture and has captured urban space in much the same way as boutiques have invaded the streets of SoHo.

Architecture for Fashion

Given that the relationship between architecture and fashion is very close in both theory and practice, how much closer must the relationship between fashion and architecture for fashion be? Architecture for fashion encompasses a broad spectrum of building typologies of which architects design only a few. Generally speaking little architectural attention is devoted to production and a great deal to sales, and the poor conditions under which fashion is produced in southern Asian and South American sweatshops are willingly ignored. There mainly women and children – the real fashion victims – work without social or legal security in intolerable conditions to sustain our dream of the democratisation of fashion. The presentations of the clothes at the fashion shows in Paris, Milan and New York occupy a special position between production and sales, as their design is often entrusted to specialists in the ephemeral such as stage designers and stylists. Therefore only a fraction of the marketing and sales process interests us here. But this is the fraction that counts in the fashion world. We should not assume that entrusting the fitting-out of fashion shops to architects is an invention of the late twentieth century. Adolf Loos' first and most important clients in Vienna were exclusive gentlemen's outfitters. The firm of Goldman und Salatsch commissioned his famous and once notorious building on Michaelerplatz that was subsequently to write architectural history, and the imperial and royal court supplier Knize – that also supplied His Imperial Majesty's unmentionables – was among Loos' first clients. Until the late 1950s the character of such commissions changed little. The primary task was to create a pleasant environment in which expensive items of clothing could be selected, tried on and sold in an atmosphere of complete calm.

The sweeping democratisation of fashion since the 1950s has also changed the shop space. The decision to buy was no longer made between products one could afford and those one could not, but became a question of self-portrayal. And shops naturally had to reflect this fact; the issue was how to translate the style of fashion into the language of architecture. The interiors had to resemble the surroundings in which the clothing would, ideally, be worn, thus allowing the customer to examine the overall effect while shopping: therefore cool sneakers were set in an exclusive, run-down club atmosphere and an evening dress by Dior was presented in a marble setting beneath crystal

Adolf Loos, Goldman & Salatsch Building, Vienna, Austria 1909–11

chandeliers – and never the other way around. This applied above all to the labels that devoted themselves to understatement: cool avant-garde clothing by Comme des Garçons with a loft feeling and designs by Vivienne Westwood in shops with names like "Too Fast to Live. Too Young to Die." In the 1990s a kind of exclusive minimalism dominated the scene that was given the name "boutique Cistercianism", as its high priest, John Pawson, was inspired by the spartan architecture of Cistercian monasticism. Starting in SoHo these highly monumental interiors with their stringent and restrained use of colour and discreetly expensive materials conquered the fashion world. The most successful pairings in this minimalist field were John Pawson/Calvin Klein, Claudio Silvestrin/Giorgio Armani and David Chipperfield/Dolce & Gabbana. Architecture critic Deyan Sudjic describes this interplay of label and architecture: "In such a setting fashion looked as if it mattered, as if it were worth the money". This kind of minimalist presentation originated from the conversion of a warehouse for the non-profit exhibition space, Dia Center for the Arts, by New York architect Richard Gluckman, who had previously worked closely with artists such as Dan Flavin and Donald Judd. The sense of awe initially employed by the designer to allow an artwork the maximum room to exert its effect was now utilised to display a black roll-neck pullover.

Günther Domenig, Humanic Shoe Shop, Vienna, Austria 1979–80

Whereas the "boutique Cistercianism" of the 1990s sought to profit from architecture's aspirations to eternity, a different trend has clearly emerged since the beginning of the new millennium: architecture is increasingly adapting itself to fashion. This is due on the one hand to the fact that clothing remains an enormous growth market, which explains why architects so thankfully accept commissions from the fashion business. On the other hand this new phenomenon also reflects the fact that our city centres are increasingly being used mono-functionally as shopping centres, as Rem Koolhaas, using very diverse examples, has analysed with his team in his extensive study "Harvard Design School Guide to Shopping" of 2001. The commissions grow increasingly larger and therefore also more challenging. In earlier days architectural shop commissions were either for a department store that sold a seemingly endless number of different products or boutiques that, although reserved exclusively for fashion, were rather puny commissions. But more recently this challenge has taken the form of building 26-storey flagship stores – such as Christian de Portzamparc's Louis Vuitton Möet Hennessy Tower – on the

Tadao Ando, 'Fabrica', Benetton Communications Research Center, Treviso, Italy 1992–2000

most famous shopping promenades of the world's most important cities, while the latest trend is the creation of "epicentres". In terms of volume the commissions have become more attractive, while at the same time fashion houses now attach more importance to obtaining the kind of architecture that is not only magnificent but also avant-garde in return for their substantial investment. Increasingly, so-called star architects are commissioned who are called upon not merely, as in previous times, to supply a generously dimensioned, luxuriously fitted ambiance but to also give the fashion houses an architectural image. The hope here, naturally, is that such buildings will function like top-class advertising in attracting attention in the confusion of the modern city, but the labels also want to emphasise their cultural aspirations more strongly; hence they engage in a kind of cultural sponsoring on their own behalf. "The wish is to utilise architecture as an advertising instrument for the label", says David McNulty, head of the architecture department at Louis Vuitton. "We have done this, but so have Prada and Hermès – and these houses have the financial means to try out new ideas in architecture." The issue here is not only advertising in the elementary and direct sense but working on branding (i.e. building up a label) to help shape the identity of a business that can then be used in its advertising.

"It's not all about branding" Rem Koolhaas

No other fashion house embodies the successful use of branding through architecture as clearly as the Milan label Prada. The decision to utilise avant-garde architecture dates from 1999 and was soon followed by commissions to OMA Office for Metropolitan Architecture, the Swiss duo Jacques Herzog and Pierre de Meuron and the young Japanese team Kazuyo Sejima and Ryue Nishizawa of SANAA. The architectural investments in this great global game are the so-called "epicentres" in New York, Tokyo, Los Angeles and San Francisco (that three of these four epicentres are in cities notoriously threatened by earthquakes is certainly part of this clever presentation). "The epicentres provide locations of concentrated creativity while Prada's familiar green boutiques will continue to stand as familiar outposts. The green stores provide a consistent image, while the scale and strategic placement of the epicentres allow them to accommodate more products, more variation and to be site specific."
The first of these centres intended to shake the fashion world was built by OMA Office for Metropolitan Architecture in New York. And it shows – like few other flagship stores – what the range of this new typology could be. Koolhaas attempts to ride

the tiger and thus hits the neuralgic nerve of the Prada customers, for he integrates what the fashion houses long ago expelled from the streets of SoHo, namely culture. At night the epicentre can be converted into a stage. In an interview with Charles Jencks the master of architectural branding admits: "It's basically to begin to re-enrich the area, since shopping is now so pervasive there. The one experience it doesn't offer is that of the public and strictly non-commercial realms. I think it's interesting to try to introduce them". This idea combines nicely with Miuccia Prada's intention to make the Fondazione Prada in Milan into an intellectual and cultural centre. While it is true that other firms also operate cultural sponsoring, in no other case is this commitment as closely integrated in the branding, nor does it seem quite so convincing elsewhere. In the meantime two further epicentres have been completed, in Tokyo and Los Angeles. The Japanese branch was designed by the Basel practice Herzog & de Meuron as a crystalline all-over display. The epicentre on Rodeo Drive in Los Angeles is again by Koolhaas, who is also working on a further one for San

Francisco. The Japanese office SANAA designed the shop-in-shop architecture where the Prada cosmetics line is retailed. The fact that two of "their" architects – Koolhaas and Herzog & de Meuron – were later awarded the Pritzker Prize, the Nobel Prize for architecture so to speak, must surely confirm to Prada that they made the correct choice. The successful architectural branding of Prada is marked by a willingness to engage in architectural experiment that makes this brand seem stronger than others who attempt to fix themselves in the customers' minds by using the same kind of architecture worldwide. "Prada represents for us a new type of client who is interested in an innovative type of architecture. This approach involves an exchange of experience and a cultural debate," said Jacques Herzog and Pierre de Meuron in fulsome praise of their client. The new organisation of the conditions of retailing also involved the development of a virtual shopping environment by AMO (an anagram and the think tank of OMA) that not only had to design the contents of the website but also to integrate the hardware in the shops. This was done with a

Massimiliano Fuksas and Doriana O. Mandrelli, Emporio Armani, Hong Kong, China 2001–02

OMA Office for Metropolitan Architecture, Prada Epicenter, New York, USA 1999–2001

certain wit and self-irony as evidenced by the LCD monitors in Los Angeles that hang from clothes hooks between the garments.

It's All about Not Branding

But there is no trend without a counter trend. Confronted with steel and glass palaces a number of fashion designers decided on strategies that were less financially expensive and publicly effective but that appeal directly to a well-off sector of fashion shoppers – mostly creative persons and intellectuals. The uncontested pioneering role here has been played for decades by Rei Kawakubo and her label Comme des Garçons. Kawakubo's approach to the design of her shop architecture is far more personal than that of Miuccia Prada. She has always been extremely involved in selecting the location and the fittings and in a certain sense used her house architect Takao Kawasaki as a means of translating her ideas. The very sparsely furnished spaces often emanate an aesthetic of non finito. But during the 1990s there was a phase in which Kawakubo attracted attention with strong architectural signals. In 1998 the collaboration with the English practice Future Systems produced the famous entrance sculpture of the shop in SoHo in New York. The Red Shop in Paris designed by Shona Kitchen and Abe Rogers in collaboration with Kawakubo opened in 2001. But this phase now seems to be over. As nowadays so many fashion houses are putting their money on architecture Rei Kawakubo has withdrawn from this arena. The new concept is guerrilla stores that open for a certain period in unusual locations in the major

cities of the world (to date Barcelona, Berlin, Warsaw and Cologne) and, after a certain length of time, close down again. Existing vacant spaces are taken over and after the allotted time has elapsed they are left again – without having been altered. There is no externally visible advertising; information is circulated by flyers, newspapers and the Internet. This is a further example of an approach that derives its inspiration from contemporary art, for example from the performances held at spectacular locations or from underground galleries. This gives customers the feeling that they are profiting from a special opportunity distant from the humdrum banality of everyday life. The strategy employed by the Dover Street Market that opened in 2004 is slightly more conventional. Here Kawakubo presents her own work and selected objects by other designers in different kinds of ephemeral inserted display elements. It is intended as a kind of market hall for exquisite things, a bazaar for unusual fashion. In much the same way as anti-advertising is itself a kind of advertising, when done as consciously as in the case of Comme des Garçons the rejection of architectural branding can in fact be used to strengthen a brand. And this message is correctly interpreted by potential customers, people who take a critical view of unbridled mass consumption. It is precisely this criticism that is instrumentalised to intellectually enrich the brand, which in turn has a positive effect on the company's balance sheets.

It is probably no accident that behind the two labels with the most interesting strategies are women who arrived at fashion by a roundabout route: Miuccia Prada studied political science and was active in the left-wing Milan theatre scene and the women's movement, while Rei Kawakubo originally studied art.

The Future of Shopping Architecture

Flagship store, ambassador shop or even epicentre: the nomenclature of these buildings is adopted from shipping, diplomacy and geology, all of which are traditionally global phenomena. We are seeing here the formation of a new architectural type. It differs from the traditional department store in that the range of goods on sale is restricted to those from a single firm while the palette of services offered is widened. However, the economic basis for this new opulence is not the fashion itself and most certainly not haute couture but rather an expanded range of casual wear, perfume, jewellery etc., which in the case of Giorgio Armani even includes chocolates and flowers. These are all often sold within a single flagship store and provide the essential turnover.

The idea is that shopping today must become a "shopping experience". With this aim in mind spectacular architecture is employed on the one hand while on the other an expanded range in the so-called "tertiary sector" is offered under a single roof, like in Colette styledesignartfood Paris – one of the first so-called concept stores. There under just one roof you can not only buy an entire lifestyle, ranging from clothes to fashion to books and suitable CDs but you can afterwards enjoy a suitably styled lunch without having to put a foot outside the shop. These days no flagship store worthy of the name can dare do without a bar, lounge or restaurant. Even luxury garages, exhibition spaces and gardens are employed at places to round off the "shopping experience". According to philanthropic press releases the general public should also be allowed to profit from these facilities, and we can only hope that the general public has enough chutzpah to drop into Prada and Co. some time with little intention

of buying anything. Architects and designers develop architectural gadgets for the shops: revolving spiral staircases, upholstered lounge areas with a TV and bar in the lift are intended to make the customers' stay more stimulating and thus to stimulate their spending, too. Many concepts also envisage places to retreat to, chill out areas, lounges where customers can recover from the exhausting business of trying on clothes shielded from the advances of eager sales staff. The electronic surveillance of customers and goods makes this apparently relaxed approach possible. The previously criminally neglected area of the changing rooms has also benefited from the new aspirations of "experience shopping". They have become dressing rooms in which customers can not only take a refreshing drink but can obtain further information about the items of clothing they are trying on via Internet. Cameras deliver simultaneous images from all sides of the garment on its wearer, finally making all that tedious twisting and turning in front of the mirror unnecessary.

The youngest generation of flagship stores and boutiques contributes to preparing the path for a new opulence that only ten years ago would have required a laborious theoretical justification but that is now emerging in the area of fashion in a far less burdened and almost brazen way. Naturally, this new revelling in forms and materials is in many cases initiated by the clients but it is impossible to ignore the obvious delight with which many architects accept this verdict. On entering such buildings one is once again permitted to laugh, even if one's smile quickly freezes on reflecting about the contexts in which architecture and fashion – and therefore architecture for fashion – are created within the global market

In this light the flagship stores could be as paradigmatic for architecture in the first years of the third millennium as new museum buildings were in the 1980s. Just as use of symbols was once again permitted in the framework of cultural institutions, in the context of buildings for fashion the repertoire of forms and materials has expanded perceptibly. Many of the projects presented in this volume illustrate the same fashion-inspired themes: revealing and concealing is clearly one of the most important leitmotifs, changing the nature of facades by the use of light and moving elements is another. These are themes that will also find an application in different, broader contexts.

Future Systems, Comme des Garçons, New York, USA 1998

Selected Bibliography

Raul A. Barrenche, New Retail, London: Phaidon, 2005.

Neil Bingham, The New Boutique: Fashion and Design, London: Merrell, 2005.

Llorenç Bonet, Cool Shops Paris, Kempen: teNeues, 2005.

Helen Castle, ed., Fashion + Architecture, Architectural Design vol. 70, no. 6, December 2000, London: Wiley-Academy.

Chuihua Judy Chung, Jeffrey Inaba, Rem Koolhaas, Sze Tsung Leong, The Harvard Design School Guide to Shopping: Harvard Design School Project on the City 2, Taschen: Cologne, 2002.

Aurora Cuito, Cool Shops London, Kempen: teNeues, 2005.

Eleanor Curtis, Fashion Retail, London: Wiley-Academy, 2003.

Corrina Dean, The Inspired Retail Space: Attract Customers, Build Branding, Increase Volume, Gloucester: Rockport Publishers, 2003.

Paula Deitz, "Luxury mirage. A new Louis Vuitton store in Tokyo's Roppongi Hills is a homage to sensuous material and optical effects", in: The Architectural Review vol. 216, 2004, p. 84–87.

Deborah Fausch et. al., ed., Architecture: In Fashion, Princeton: Princeton Architectural Press, 1994.

Maria Luisa Frisa, Mario Lupano, Stefano Tonchi, eds, Total Living: Art, Fashion, Design, Architecture, Communication, Milan: Edizioni Charta, 2002.

Jacques Herzog, Pierre de Meuron, Miuccia Prada, Patrizio Bertelli, Prada Aoyama Tokyo, Milan: Fondazione Prada, 2004.

Inclusive: The Architecture of Louis Vuitton, exhibition catalogue, Berlin: Aedes 2003.

Falk Jaeger, Rudi Baur, adidas factory outlet, Ludwigsburg: av-edition, 2004.

Caroline Klein, Cool Shops Milan, Kempen: teNeues, 2005.

Rem Koolhaas, Miuccia Prada, Patrizio Bertelli, Projects for Prada Part 1, Milan: Fondazione Prada, 2001.

Ian Luna, Retail: Architecture + Shopping, New York: Rizzoli, 2005.

Wakato Onishi, "New Century Modern" (Toyo Ito, Tod's, Tokyo), in: domus, February 2005, p. 14–25.

Bradley Quinn, The Fashion of Architecture, Oxford: Berg Publishers, 2004.

Valerie Steele, ed., Encyclopedia of Clothing and Fashion, 3 vols. Detroit/London: Thomson Gale, 2005.

Deyan Sudjic, Rei Kawakubo and Comme des Garçons, New York: Rizzoli, 1990.

Deyan Sudjic, "Cultura e mercato" (Herzog & de Meuron, Prada Tokyo), in: domus, July/August 2003, p. 45–50.

Sophie Trelcat, "Siège social de la maison du couture Jean-Paul Gaultier, Paris, Alain Moatti et Henri Rivière architects", in: L'architecture d'aujourd'hui, vol. 354, 2004, p. 22–24.

Kazys Varnelis, "Architecture after Couture", in: Thresholds, summer 2001.

Désirée von la Valette, Cool Shops New York, Kempen: teNeues, 2005.

Peter Wollen, Fiona Bradley, eds, Addressing the Century: 100 Years of Art & Fashion, exhibition catalogue, London: Hayward Gallery, 1998.